Book About Changing Schools

Crafted by Skriuwer

Table of Contents

Chapter 1

Why Do Kids Change Schools?

Moving to a New House

Moving to a new house can be both an exciting and challenging experience for children. It is a significant life event that can impact a child's social, emotional, and academic well-being. This section delves into the various aspects of how this transition can affect children and provides guidance on how to navigate this change successfully.

Impact of Moving to a New House

When a family decides to move to a new house, children may experience a range of emotions. Some children may feel excited about the prospect of a new home, while others may feel anxious or sad about leaving their current surroundings. Moving to a new house can disrupt a child's sense of stability and familiarity, as they have to adjust to a new neighborhood, school, and routine.

Preparing for the Move

Before the actual move takes place, it is essential for parents to involve their children in the process. This can include discussing the reasons for the move, visiting the new neighborhood, and involving children in packing decisions. By involving children in the moving process, parents can help alleviate some of the anxiety and uncertainty that children may be feeling.

Saying Goodbye

As the moving day approaches, it is important for children to have the opportunity to say goodbye to their current home, neighborhood, and friends. Planning a goodbye party or gathering can allow children to express their emotions and create lasting memories. Collecting contact information from friends and teachers can help children stay connected even after the move.

Adjusting to the New Environment

Once the move is complete, children will need time to adjust to their new house and surroundings. Parents can support their children by helping them get acquainted with the new neighborhood, school, and community. Visiting the new school before the first day can help ease some of the anxiety about starting in a new environment.

Maintaining a Positive Attitude

Throughout the moving process, it is essential for children to maintain a positive attitude. Encouraging children to focus on the opportunities and adventures that come with moving to a new house can help them embrace the change with optimism. Reminding children that change is a natural part of life and that they have the strength and resilience to adapt can empower them to face the challenges of moving.

In conclusion, moving to a new house is a significant transition for children that can bring about a mix of emotions. By involving children in the moving process, allowing them to say goodbye to their old home, and supporting them as they adjust to their new environment, parents can help children navigate this change successfully. Encouraging a positive attitude and emphasizing the opportunities for growth and new experiences can help children embrace the journey of moving to a new house with confidence and resilience.

Parents' Job Changes

Parents' job changes can be a significant reason why kids have to change schools. In today's fast-paced world, career opportunities often require families to relocate to a new city or even a different country. This can be a challenging transition for children as they have to leave behind their familiar school environment and friends. In this section, we will explore the impact of parents' job changes on children and provide tips on how to navigate this change effectively.

When parents' job changes necessitate a move to a new location, children may experience a range of emotions. They might feel excited about the prospect of exploring a new place and making new friends, but they may also feel anxious about leaving their current school and friends behind. It is essential for parents to acknowledge and validate their children's feelings during this time of transition.

One of the key challenges that children face when changing schools due to parents' job changes is adjusting to a new school environment. They may feel overwhelmed by the unfamiliar faces, routines, and expectations of their new school. To help children prepare for this change, parents can involve them in the decision-making process by discussing the reasons for the move and addressing any concerns or questions they may have.

Visiting the new school before the move can also help ease children's transition. Parents can schedule a tour of the school, meet with teachers and staff, and explore the campus together. This can help children feel more comfortable and familiar with their new surroundings before their first day.

It is important for parents to communicate openly with their children about the changes that come with parents' job changes. They can reassure their children that they will support them through this transition and help them navigate any challenges that may arise. Encouraging children to express their thoughts and feelings can help them process their emotions and adapt to their new school environment more effectively.

Parents can also help children stay connected with their old friends after changing schools due to parents' job changes. Encouraging children to maintain relationships with their previous classmates through social media, phone calls, or visits can provide them with a sense of continuity and support during this period of change.

In conclusion, parents' job changes can have a significant impact on children's schooling experiences. By acknowledging their children's feelings, involving them in the transition process, and providing them with support and reassurance, parents can help their children navigate this change successfully. With patience, understanding, and open communication, children can adapt to their new school environment and thrive in their academic and social pursuits.

Going to a Different Grade Level

Transitioning to a new grade level can be both an exciting and daunting experience for students. As they progress through their educational journey, they are faced with new challenges, expectations, and opportunities. In this chapter, we will explore the significance of moving up to a different grade level and provide guidance on how to navigate this important transition.

Understanding the Transition

Moving to a different grade level marks a significant milestone in a student's academic career. Whether it's transitioning from elementary to middle school or from middle school to high school, each grade level change brings about a new set of expectations and responsibilities. Students are not only introduced to more complex academic concepts but also to a different social environment that may require them to adapt and grow.

One of the key reasons why students change grade levels is to continue their educational progression and development. Each grade level is designed to build upon the knowledge and skills acquired in the previous one, providing students with a more comprehensive and challenging learning experience. Moving up to a higher grade level signifies that students are ready to take on new academic challenges and expand their horizons.

Preparing for the Change

Preparing for the transition to a different grade level is essential to ensure a smooth adjustment. Students can start by familiarizing themselves with the curriculum and expectations of the new grade level. This may involve researching the subjects they will be studying, understanding the grading system, and identifying any areas where they may need additional support.

Visiting the school and meeting with teachers can also help students feel more comfortable and prepared for the transition. By getting to know their new learning environment and the individuals who will be guiding them through the academic year, students can alleviate some of the anxiety associated with starting a new grade level.

Maintaining a Positive Attitude

Approaching the transition with a positive attitude can make a significant difference in how students perceive and adapt to the change. Encouraging students to embrace the opportunities that come with moving to a different grade level, such as meeting new classmates, exploring new subjects, and participating in extracurricular activities, can help them feel more excited and optimistic about the transition.

It's important for students to recognize that it's normal to feel a mix of emotions when starting a new grade level. Whether they feel nervous, excited, or unsure, acknowledging and expressing their feelings can help them process their emotions and seek support from trusted adults or peers.

Embracing Growth and Learning

Moving to a different grade level is a significant step towards personal and academic growth. Students have the opportunity to challenge themselves, discover new interests, and develop valuable skills that will benefit them in the future. By staying open-minded, curious, and resilient, students can make the most of their experience at the new grade level and continue to thrive academically and personally.

In conclusion, going to a different grade level is a pivotal moment in a student's educational journey. By understanding the significance of this transition, preparing for the change, maintaining a positive attitude, and embracing growth and learning, students can navigate this important milestone with confidence and enthusiasm.

Finding a School That Fits You Better

Choosing a school that fits you better involves considering several factors that can contribute to your overall well-being and academic success. It's essential to assess your unique learning style, interests, and goals to determine the type of educational environment that will support your growth and development.

One of the key aspects to consider when finding a school that fits you better is the academic programs and curriculum offered. Different schools may have varying approaches to teaching and learning, so it's essential to explore the educational opportunities available at each institution. Consider whether the school offers courses that align with your interests and career aspirations, as well as extracurricular activities that can enhance your overall learning experience.

Another important factor to consider is the school's size and culture. Some students thrive in smaller, more intimate learning environments where they can receive personalized attention from teachers, while others may prefer larger schools with a diverse student body and a wide range of resources. Reflect on your social preferences and comfort level to determine the type of school community that will best support your academic and personal growth.

Furthermore, it's crucial to consider the location and facilities of the school. Evaluate factors such as the school's proximity to your home, transportation options, and the quality of the campus facilities. A school that is conveniently located and provides a conducive learning environment can contribute to your overall academic success and well-being.

When exploring different schools, don't hesitate to visit the campuses and speak with current students, teachers, and administrators to gain insights into the school's culture and values. Ask questions about the school's academic programs, extracurricular offerings, support services, and opportunities for personal and professional growth.

Additionally, consider seeking input from trusted adults, such as parents, teachers, or guidance counselors, who can provide valuable guidance and advice as you navigate the process of finding a school that fits you better. They can offer valuable insights based on their knowledge and experience, helping you make an informed decision that aligns with your academic and personal goals.

In conclusion, finding a school that fits you better is a personalized and reflective process that requires careful consideration of your individual needs, interests, and goals. By taking the time to evaluate different schools and assess how they align with your academic and personal preferences, you can make an informed decision that sets the foundation for a positive and fulfilling educational experience.

Chapter 2

Preparing for the Big Move

Telling Your Friends and Teachers

Moving to a new school can be both exciting and nerve-wracking, especially when it comes to informing your friends and teachers about the big change. The transition may bring about mixed emotions, but it's important to handle this step with care and consideration. In this chapter, we will discuss the significance of informing your friends and teachers, the best ways to go about it, and how to prepare yourself for the reactions you may encounter.

Telling Your Friends:
One of the first things you'll want to do when preparing for a move to a new school is to inform your friends. They have likely been a significant part of your life, and sharing this news with them can help maintain your bond even if you'll be physically apart. It's important to be honest and open with your friends about the move, as keeping them in the loop will allow for a smoother transition.

Consider setting up a time to talk with your friends in person or via video call if they are not nearby. Express your feelings about the move and let them know how much their friendship means to you. Reassure them that distance won't change your connection and that you'll make an effort to stay in touch. Encourage them to share their feelings as well and address any concerns they may have about your departure.

Telling Your Teachers:
Informing your teachers about your impending move is also crucial, as they play a significant role in your academic and emotional well-being. Approach this conversation respectfully and professionally, expressing gratitude for their support and guidance throughout your time at the current school. Let them know about your move and discuss the timeline for your departure.

It's essential to ask your teachers for any advice or recommendations they may have for your transition to a new school. They may be able to provide valuable insights or connect you with resources that can help ease the process. Keep the lines of communication open with your teachers as you prepare to leave, and thank them for their understanding and assistance during this period of change.

Preparing Yourself:
As you navigate the process of telling your friends and teachers about your move, it's normal to experience a range of emotions, including sadness, excitement, and anxiety. Take time to process your feelings and be kind to yourself as you navigate this transition. Remember that change is a natural part of life, and while saying goodbye can be difficult, it also opens the door to new opportunities and experiences.

Stay connected with your friends and teachers even after you've moved to your new school. Make an effort to maintain those relationships through regular communication, whether it's through social media, emails, or visits during holidays. Embrace the memories you've shared with your friends and teachers at your old school, and carry those experiences with you as you embark on this new chapter in your educational journey.

In conclusion, telling your friends and teachers about your move to a new school is an important step in the transition process. By approaching these conversations with honesty, compassion, and gratitude, you can maintain strong connections with those who have been a part of your support system. Remember that change brings growth and new opportunities, and that staying connected with old friends and mentors can enrich your experiences both at your current school and in your future endeavors.

Visiting Your New School

Visiting your new school is an important step in preparing for the big move. It allows you to familiarize yourself with the campus, meet some of the staff and students, and start to feel more comfortable in your new environment. This chapter will guide you through the process of visiting your new school and making the most out of this experience.

1. Schedule a Tour: Before your official first day at the new school, it's a good idea to schedule a tour of the campus. This can usually be arranged through the school's administration office. During the tour, you will have the opportunity to see the classrooms, library, cafeteria, gym, and other important areas of the school. Pay attention to the layout of the building and ask questions about any areas you are curious about.

2. Meet the Staff: During your visit, you may have the chance to meet some of the teachers, counselors, and other staff members. Take this opportunity to introduce yourself, ask questions about the school, and get to know the people who will be supporting you in your new academic journey. Building positive relationships with the staff can help you feel more comfortable and supported in your new school environment.

3. Explore Extracurricular Activities: While visiting the school, ask about the extracurricular activities and clubs that are available to students. These can range from sports teams to academic clubs to special interest groups. Getting involved in extracurricular activities is a great way to make friends, explore your interests, and feel more connected to the school community. Consider joining a club or team that aligns with your passions and hobbies.

4. Check Out the Facilities: Take the time to explore the school facilities during your visit. Visit the library to see what resources are available, check out the gym and sports fields, and familiarize yourself with the cafeteria and other common areas. Understanding the layout of the school and where different facilities are located can help you feel more at ease on your first day and in the weeks to come.

5. Ask Questions: Don't be afraid to ask questions during your visit. Whether you're curious about the school's academic programs, daily schedule, or student support services, the staff is there to help you navigate the transition to your new school. Be proactive in seeking information that will help you feel prepared and confident as you start this new chapter in your education.

6. Connect with Peers: If possible, try to connect with some of your future classmates during your visit to the school. Making new friends before the official start of the school year can help ease any anxiety you may be feeling about the transition. Exchange contact information with potential new friends and consider arranging a meet-up outside of school to start building those connections.

Visiting your new school is an exciting opportunity to begin acclimating to your new learning environment and start building relationships with your future classmates and teachers. By taking the time to explore the campus, meet the staff, and ask questions, you can feel more prepared and confident as you embark on this new chapter in your academic journey. Use this visit as a chance to envision yourself thriving in your new school and embrace the opportunities that lie ahead.

Learning About Your New School

One of the most important steps in preparing for a big move to a new school is taking the time to learn all about your new educational environment. By understanding the ins and outs of your new school, you can feel more confident and prepared as you transition into this new chapter of your academic journey.

First and foremost, it is essential to gather information about the basic details of the school. This includes familiarizing yourself with the school's location, layout, and facilities. Take a virtual tour of the school's website or reach out to the school administration to request a school map. Knowing where important areas such as the main office, classrooms, cafeteria, gym, and library are located can help ease any anxiety about navigating the school on your first day.

Next, research the academic programs and extracurricular activities offered at your new school. Understanding the curriculum and learning opportunities available can give you a sense of what to expect in terms of coursework and potential areas of interest to explore. Look into clubs, sports teams, and special programs that align with your interests and consider how you can get involved and make the most of your time at the school.

It is also important to learn about the school's culture and values. Every school has its unique atmosphere and community, so take the time to read about the school's mission statement, values, and any initiatives they may have in place. Understanding the school's culture can help you adapt more easily and connect with your peers and teachers on a deeper level.

Additionally, reach out to current students or alumni of the school to gain insights into their experiences. Connecting with others who have attended or are currently attending the school can provide valuable information and tips on how to thrive in your new environment. Ask about the academic rigor, social dynamics, and any advice they may have for new students.

Furthermore, familiarize yourself with the school's policies and procedures. This includes understanding the school's code of conduct, attendance policies, dress code, and any other rules that may impact your daily school life. Being aware of these guidelines can help you avoid any misunderstandings or conflicts and ensure a smooth transition into the school community.

Lastly, consider scheduling a visit to the school before your official first day. This can give you the opportunity to walk around the campus, meet some staff members, and get a feel for the overall atmosphere of the school. By physically immersing yourself in the school environment beforehand, you can start to visualize yourself as a part of the community and build excitement for the new chapter ahead.

In conclusion, learning about your new school is a crucial step in preparing for a successful transition. By taking the time to gather information about the school's location, programs, culture, and policies, you can feel more confident and ready to embrace the opportunities that await you. Remember that every new school brings with it a chance for growth and new experiences, so approach this learning process with curiosity and an open mind.

Packing Up Your School Supplies

As you prepare for the big move to your new school, one important task that you will need to tackle is packing up your school supplies. This may seem like a simple and straightforward task, but taking the time to organize and pack your belongings carefully can help ease the transition to your new environment. In this section, we will explore the importance of packing up your school supplies and provide you with some tips on how to make this process more efficient and stress-free.

1. Organizing Your School Supplies:

Before you start packing, take some time to organize your school supplies. Sort through your belongings and separate them into categories such as textbooks, notebooks, pens, pencils, and other stationery items. Having a clear idea of what you have will make it easier to pack efficiently and ensure that you have everything you need for your new school.

2. Packing Methodically:

When it comes to packing your school supplies, it's essential to be methodical. Start by gathering all the items you will need, such as backpacks, pencil cases, and storage containers. Pack heavier items at the bottom of your bag to prevent them from crushing more delicate items. Use zip-lock bags or small containers to store smaller items like erasers or paper clips to prevent them from getting lost.

3. Labeling Your Supplies:

To make unpacking easier once you arrive at your new school, consider labeling your school supplies. Use sticky notes or labels to mark boxes or containers with the contents inside. This way, you can quickly identify where each item belongs without having to rummage through all your belongings.

4. Essential Items Checklist:

Make a checklist of essential items that you will need for your first day at your new school. This may include textbooks, notebooks, pens, pencils, erasers, rulers, and any other materials required for your classes. By double-checking your list, you can ensure that you have everything you need to start the school year off on the right foot.

5. Organization Systems:

Consider implementing organization systems to keep your school supplies tidy and easily accessible. Invest in a sturdy backpack with compartments to store your books and notebooks separately. Use pencil cases or pouches to keep your pens, pencils, and other stationery items organized. Having a system in place will make it easier for you to find what you need quickly during the school day.

6. Packing Up Emotionally:

While packing up your school supplies, you may also experience a range of emotions as you prepare to leave your familiar environment behind. Take this opportunity to reflect on the memories you have made at your current school and acknowledge any feelings of sadness or nostalgia that may arise. Remember that it's okay to feel a mix of emotions during this transition period.

Packing up your school supplies is an essential step in preparing for your move to a new school. By taking the time to organize your belongings, pack methodically, and label your supplies, you can make the transition smoother and more manageable. Remember to stay positive and embrace this new chapter in your academic journey with an open mind and a willingness to adapt to new experiences.

Keeping a Positive Attitude

Maintaining a positive attitude begins with understanding that change is a natural part of life and can lead to new opportunities and growth. It is normal to feel a mix of emotions when facing a school transition, including excitement, nervousness, and sadness. Acknowledging these feelings and accepting them as part of the process is the first step towards cultivating positivity.

One effective way to foster a positive attitude is by focusing on the benefits and possibilities that come with changing schools. Remind yourself of the new experiences, friendships, and learning opportunities that await you at your new school. Embrace the chance to start fresh and explore different aspects of yourself in a new environment.

Another key aspect of maintaining a positive attitude is staying optimistic and hopeful about the future. Visualize a successful transition and imagine yourself thriving in your new school. Positive visualization can help alleviate anxiety and boost confidence as you prepare for the changes ahead.

Practicing gratitude is a powerful tool for cultivating positivity during challenging times. Take time each day to reflect on the things you are grateful for, whether it's supportive friends and family, exciting opportunities, or personal strengths. Gratitude can shift your focus from uncertainties to blessings, fostering a sense of optimism and resilience.

It is also important to surround yourself with positivity during the transition period. Seek support from friends, family, teachers, or counselors who can offer encouragement and reassurance. Engage in activities that bring you joy and relaxation, such as hobbies, exercise, or spending time in nature. Creating a supportive and uplifting environment can help you navigate the changes with a positive mindset.

Lastly, practicing self-care and self-compassion is essential for maintaining a positive attitude during times of transition. Be kind to yourself, acknowledge your efforts and progress, and allow yourself to feel a range of emotions without judgment. Taking care of your physical, emotional, and mental well-being will help you stay resilient and optimistic throughout the school change process.

In conclusion, keeping a positive attitude is a mindset that can significantly impact your experience of changing schools. By embracing change with optimism, gratitude, and self-care, you can navigate the transition smoothly and adapt successfully to your new school environment. Remember that change is an opportunity for growth and learning, and maintaining a positive outlook will empower you to make the most of your new school experience.

Chapter 3

Saying Goodbye

Planning a Goodbye Party

Saying goodbye can be a bittersweet experience, especially when leaving behind friends and memories at a school you've grown to love. Planning a goodbye party is a thoughtful way to celebrate the friendships and connections you've made before embarking on a new chapter in your life. In this chapter, we will explore the importance of planning a goodbye party, along with some tips on how to make it a memorable and meaningful event.

Why Plan a Goodbye Party?

A goodbye party serves as a farewell gathering to express gratitude, share memories, and bid adieu to friends and teachers who have been a significant part of your school journey. It provides an opportunity to create lasting memories and strengthen bonds before moving on to a new environment. Saying goodbye in a positive and celebratory manner can help ease the transition and leave a positive impression on those you are leaving behind.

Tips for Planning a Goodbye Party:

1. Choose a Date and Venue: Select a date that works for you and your friends, considering school schedules and other commitments. The venue can be at your home, a park, or a local community center, depending on the number of guests and your preferences.

2. Create Invitations: Design and send out invitations to your friends, teachers, and anyone else you would like to invite to the party. Include details such as the date, time, venue, and any special instructions or requests.

3. Plan Activities: Consider incorporating fun activities or games that will help create a lively and engaging atmosphere. You can organize a photo booth, a memory jar where guests can write messages or memories, or a slideshow of memorable moments from your time at the school.

4. Prepare Refreshments: Food and drinks are essential components of any party. Plan a menu that includes snacks, beverages, and perhaps a cake or dessert to mark the occasion. You can also consider asking guests to bring a dish to share, creating a potluck-style gathering.

5. Decorate the Space: Enhance the party atmosphere by decorating the venue with balloons, streamers, banners, and other decorations that reflect the theme of saying goodbye and moving on to new beginnings.

6. Share Memories and Photos: Encourage guests to share stories, memories, and heartfelt messages as a way to commemorate your time together. Display photos or create a memory board showcasing significant moments and milestones from your school years.

7. Express Gratitude: Take a moment during the party to express your gratitude to everyone who has been a part of your school experience. Thank your friends, teachers, and mentors for their support and friendship, and let them know how much their presence has meant to you.

8. Exchange Contact Information: Before saying goodbye, make sure to exchange contact information with your friends and teachers so you can stay connected even after you've moved to a new school. Consider creating a contact list or group chat to facilitate communication and maintain relationships.

By planning a goodbye party with care and thoughtfulness, you can create a memorable and meaningful experience that will leave a lasting impression on everyone involved. Saying goodbye is never easy, but by celebrating the past and looking forward to the future, you can transition to a new school with positivity and optimism.

Collecting Contact Information

Collecting contact information is an important aspect of transitioning to a new school. It allows you to stay connected with your old friends and teachers, maintaining those relationships even as you embark on a new chapter in your educational journey. In Chapter 3 of the book "Book about Changing Schools," the process of collecting contact information is highlighted as a key step in saying goodbye to your current school community.

When you are preparing to move to a new school, it is essential to gather the contact information of your friends, teachers, and other important figures in your current school life. This information can include email addresses, phone numbers, social media handles, and mailing addresses. By collecting this information, you can ensure that you can stay in touch with the people who have been a significant part of your life up to this point.

One way to collect contact information is to organize a farewell gathering or party. This provides a fun and informal setting for you to exchange contact details with your friends and teachers. You can create a contact list where everyone can write down their information, or you can simply exchange phone numbers and social media handles with those you want to stay connected with.

Another way to collect contact information is to create a digital contact list. You can use a spreadsheet or a contact management app to input the information of your friends and teachers. This digital list makes it easy to keep track of everyone's contact details and ensures that you have all the information you need to stay connected.

In addition to collecting contact information, it is also important to share your own contact details with others. Make sure to give your friends and teachers your new contact information so that they can reach out to you once you have moved to your new school. This reciprocity ensures that the lines of communication remain open both ways, allowing for continued connections and friendships to flourish.

It is important to remember that saying goodbye and collecting contact information can be an emotional process. You may feel sad about leaving behind the familiar faces and routines of your current school. However, by collecting contact information and staying connected with your old friends and teachers, you can ease the transition and maintain those important relationships even from a distance.

In conclusion, collecting contact information is a vital part of saying goodbye to your current school community as you prepare to move to a new school. By gathering the contact details of your friends and teachers, you can stay connected and continue to nurture those relationships even as you embark on a new educational journey. Remember that change can be challenging, but with the support of your old friends and teachers, you can navigate this transition with grace and positivity.

Sharing Memories and Photos

One of the key elements of bidding farewell to your old school and friends is sharing memories and photos. This section touches on the significance of reminiscing about the past while also looking forward to exciting new opportunities.

Collecting Contact Information: Before embarking on your new school journey, it's essential to collect contact information from your friends and teachers at your current school. This way, you can stay in touch and maintain those valuable connections even after the physical distance between you grows. Exchange email addresses, phone numbers, and social media handles to ensure you can easily reach out and share updates with one another.

Planning a Goodbye Party: Hosting a goodbye party is a wonderful way to gather your friends and teachers to celebrate the time you've spent together. It's a chance to reminisce about fun moments, express gratitude for the friendships you've formed, and create lasting memories. Encourage everyone to bring photos or mementos to share, adding a special touch to the farewell event.

Sharing Memories and Photos: During the goodbye party or in the days leading up to your move, take the opportunity to share memories and photos with your friends. Reflect on significant events, funny anecdotes, and meaningful experiences you've shared together. Looking at old photos can evoke emotions and strengthen the bond you have with your peers, creating a sense of nostalgia and unity.

Understanding That It's Okay to Feel Sad: Saying goodbye can be an emotional experience, and it's important to acknowledge and process those feelings. It's natural to feel sad about leaving behind familiar faces and routines. By sharing memories and photos, you validate the impact your friends have had on your life and honor the connections you've built. Allow yourself to feel the emotions that come with saying goodbye while also embracing the excitement of new beginnings.

Staying Connected with Old Friends: As you transition to your new school, make a conscious effort to stay connected with your old friends. Utilize technology to maintain communication through messaging apps, social media platforms, or video calls. Share updates about your new school, adventures, and achievements to keep the bond alive despite the distance. Planning visits during holidays or breaks can also provide opportunities to reunite in person and create new memories together.

In conclusion, sharing memories and photos is a heartfelt way to cherish the relationships and experiences you've had at your old school. It allows you to honor the past, express gratitude for the friendships you've cultivated, and strengthen the connections that will endure beyond physical separation. By embracing this aspect of saying goodbye, you pave the way for a smoother transition to your new school while carrying the cherished memories of your past with you.

Understanding That It's Okay to Feel Sad

It is crucial for children to comprehend that feeling sad during this period is entirely natural and expected. Moving away from familiar surroundings, friends, and routines can evoke a range of emotions, including sadness, and it's essential for children to acknowledge and process these feelings in a healthy manner.

When a child is preparing to say goodbye to their current school and friends, they may experience a sense of loss and nostalgia. It's important to validate these emotions and let them know that it's okay to feel sad. Encouraging children to express their feelings through open communication, such as talking to parents, teachers, or friends, can help them cope with the transition more effectively.

Planning a goodbye party can also provide a constructive outlet for processing emotions. By gathering with friends and classmates to share memories and experiences, children can celebrate the time they've spent together while also acknowledging that things are changing. Collecting contact information and creating a plan to stay in touch can offer reassurance that friendships can endure despite physical distance.

Sharing memories and photos can be a therapeutic way for children to reminisce about the good times they've had at their old school. Looking back on fond memories and creating a keepsake of their time there can help children feel a sense of closure and acceptance as they prepare to move on to a new chapter in their lives.

It's crucial for children to understand that feeling sad during times of change is a natural part of the process. Encouraging them to express their emotions, seek support from trusted adults, and engage in activities that promote self-expression can help them navigate these feelings in a healthy way. Reminding children that it's okay to feel sad, and reassuring them that these emotions will eventually pass, can provide comfort and reassurance during this challenging time.

As children prepare to transition to a new school, it's important for parents, teachers, and caregivers to offer support and understanding as they navigate through the emotional ups and downs of saying goodbye. By acknowledging and validating children's feelings of sadness, we can help them develop resilience and coping skills that will serve them well in handling future changes and challenges with confidence and grace.

Staying Connected with Old Friends

As you embark on your new school journey, it's important to remember the friends you've left behind. Staying connected with old friends can provide comfort, support, and a sense of continuity as you navigate the challenges of transitioning to a new school. In this chapter, we explore various ways in which you can maintain and nurture your existing friendships, even as you make new connections in your new school environment.

Writing Letters or Emails

One timeless way to stay in touch with old friends is through written correspondence. Taking the time to write a letter or send an email can help you express your thoughts and feelings, share updates on your new school experiences, and reminisce about shared memories. Writing letters or emails allows you to maintain a personal connection with your friends, even if you're physically apart.

Video Calls and Phone Chats

In today's digital age, technology offers us convenient ways to stay connected with others, regardless of distance. Video calls and phone chats enable you to see and hear your friends in real time, making it feel as though you're right there with them. These platforms provide opportunities for meaningful conversations, laughter, and shared experiences, helping you bridge the gap between old and new friendships.

Planning Visits During Holidays

If possible, consider planning visits to see your old friends during school holidays or breaks. Spending time together in person can strengthen your bond, create new memories, and reaffirm the value of your friendship. Whether it's a day trip, a weekend getaway, or a longer vacation, these visits can be a source of joy and connection for both you and your friends.

Sharing Updates and Stories

Keeping your friends updated on your life and experiences at your new school can help them feel involved and connected to your journey. Whether it's sharing photos, recounting funny anecdotes, or discussing your challenges and triumphs, sharing updates and stories can maintain a sense of closeness and understanding between you and your old friends.

Balancing Old and New Friendships

While it's important to stay connected with your old friends, it's also essential to nurture and invest in your new friendships at your new school. Finding a balance between maintaining old friendships and cultivating new ones can enrich your social life, broaden your support network, and foster personal growth. By embracing both old and new relationships, you can create a diverse and fulfilling social circle that supports you in your transition.

In conclusion, staying connected with old friends is a meaningful and enriching aspect of the school transition process. By utilizing various communication methods, planning visits, sharing updates, and balancing relationships, you can preserve the bonds you've formed while embracing the opportunities for growth and connection in your new school environment. Remember, friendships are valuable connections that can span time and distance, and nurturing them can bring joy, support, and a sense of belonging to your life.

Chapter 4

First Day at Your New School

Getting Ready the Night Before

Preparing for your first day at a new school is an exciting but nerve-wracking experience. One of the keys to ensuring a smooth transition is getting ready the night before. By taking some time to prepare in advance, you can alleviate some of the stress and anxiety that often comes with starting at a new school. Here are some tips on how to get ready the night before your big day:

1. Organize Your Supplies: Take some time to gather all the necessary school supplies you will need for your first day. Make sure you have your notebooks, pens, pencils, textbooks, and any other materials required for your classes. Having everything organized and ready to go will help you feel more prepared and confident.

2. Choose Your Outfit: Selecting your outfit the night before can save you time and stress in the morning. Pick out an outfit that makes you feel comfortable and confident. Consider the dress code of your new school and choose something appropriate that reflects your personal style.

3. Pack Your Backpack: Pack your backpack with all the essentials you will need for the day. Make sure you have your school supplies, lunch, water bottle, and any other items you may need. Double-check to ensure you have everything you need for a successful first day.

4. Review Your Schedule: Take some time to review your schedule for the next day. Familiarize yourself with the times and locations of your classes, as well as any extracurricular activities or events you may have scheduled. Knowing your schedule in advance can help ease any anxiety about getting lost or being late.

5. Get a Good Night's Sleep: It's important to get a good night's sleep before your first day at a new school. Aim for at least 8 hours of rest to ensure you wake up feeling refreshed and ready to tackle the day ahead. Avoid caffeine and electronic devices before bed to help you unwind and relax.

6. Visualize a Positive Day: Before you go to sleep, take a few moments to visualize a positive and successful first day at your new school. Imagine yourself making new friends, navigating your classes with ease, and enjoying the new experiences that await you. Visualizing a positive outcome can help boost your confidence and mindset for the day ahead.

7. Stay Calm and Positive: Lastly, try to stay calm and positive as you prepare for your first day. It's normal to feel nervous or anxious about starting at a new school, but remember that you are capable and resilient. Focus on the exciting opportunities that lie ahead and approach the day with a positive attitude.

By following these tips and getting ready the night before, you can set yourself up for a successful and enjoyable first day at your new school. Remember to take deep breaths, stay organized, and embrace the new experiences and friendships that come your way. Good luck on your first day!

Finding Your Way Around

Moving to a new school can be an exciting yet daunting experience. One of the first things you'll need to do on your first day is to navigate your way around the new school. This chapter will guide you on how to find your way around and make the transition smoother.

1. Getting Ready the Night Before
Before your first day at the new school, it's essential to prepare yourself mentally and physically. Lay out your clothes, pack your backpack with all the necessary supplies, and ensure you have a good night's sleep. Feeling well-rested and organized will help you approach the day with a positive mindset.

2. Understanding the School Layout
On your first day, take some time to familiarize yourself with the school layout. Obtain a map of the school if possible, or ask for directions from teachers or staff members. Identify key areas such as classrooms, the cafeteria, the library, and restrooms. Knowing where everything is located will help you feel more confident and less overwhelmed.

3. Meeting Your New Teacher
Your teacher will be your guide and support system in the new school. Introduce yourself, ask any questions you may have, and listen attentively to the teacher's instructions. They can provide valuable information about the school and help you settle in.

4. Navigating the Hallways

Walking through the hallways can be intimidating at first, but don't be afraid to ask for directions if you get lost. Look for signs or landmarks that can help you find your way around. Remember that it's okay to take your time and explore the school at your own pace.

5. Introducing Yourself to Classmates

Making connections with your classmates is an important part of feeling comfortable in a new environment. Introduce yourself with a smile, be open to conversations, and show interest in getting to know them. Building positive relationships with your peers will make the transition smoother and more enjoyable.

6. Being Open to New Experiences

Embrace the opportunity to try new things and step out of your comfort zone. Participate in classroom activities, join clubs or sports teams, and engage in school events. By being open to new experiences, you'll not only find your way around the school but also discover your interests and passions.

Navigating your way around a new school may seem challenging at first, but with a positive attitude and willingness to explore, you'll soon feel at home in your new environment. Remember that it's okay to ask for help, take things one step at a time, and celebrate your achievements along the way. Finding your way around is just the beginning of your exciting journey at your new school.

Meeting Your New Teacher

Meeting your new teacher can be an exciting and nerve-wracking experience as you begin your journey at a new school. Your teacher plays a crucial role in shaping your academic experience and providing support as you navigate through your new environment. This chapter will guide you on how to approach this meeting with confidence and positivity.

First impressions matter, so it's essential to make a good impression when meeting your new teacher. Arrive on time, with a positive attitude, and be prepared to introduce yourself politely. Remember that your teacher is there to help you succeed and is excited to get to know you.

During your first meeting, take the opportunity to ask questions and get to know your teacher better. Inquire about their teaching style, classroom expectations, and any specific guidelines they have in place. This will help you understand what is expected of you and how to succeed in their class.

It's also essential to share information about yourself with your teacher. Let them know about your interests, strengths, and any challenges you may face. Building a positive relationship with your teacher from the beginning will make it easier for you to seek help when needed and feel supported in your academic journey.

As you interact with your new teacher, pay attention to their communication style and teaching methods. Every teacher is unique, and understanding how your teacher operates can help you adapt to their expectations and excel in their class. Be open to feedback and constructive criticism, as it will help you grow as a student and improve your academic performance.

Additionally, take the time to express your goals and aspirations to your teacher. Whether you aim to improve your grades, participate in extracurricular activities, or pursue a specific career path, sharing your ambitions with your teacher can help them support you in reaching your objectives.

Building a positive and respectful relationship with your teacher is key to your academic success. Show appreciation for their guidance and support, participate actively in class discussions, and demonstrate a willingness to learn and grow. Your teacher is there to help you succeed, so make the most of this valuable resource by engaging with them and seeking their assistance when needed.

Remember that your teacher is there to support you every step of the way. Don't hesitate to reach out to them if you have questions, concerns, or need extra help with your studies. By fostering a positive and collaborative relationship with your teacher, you can make the most of your academic experience and thrive in your new school environment.

Meeting your new teacher is an exciting opportunity to start fresh and embark on a journey of learning and growth. Approach this meeting with an open mind, a positive attitude, and a willingness to build a strong and supportive relationship with your teacher. By taking the initiative to connect with your teacher and seek their guidance, you can set yourself up for success in your academic endeavors.

Introducing Yourself to Classmates

Introducing yourself to classmates is a crucial step in settling into a new school environment. It can be both exciting and nerve-wracking as you are meeting new people who will potentially become your friends and peers for the academic year. In this chapter, we will delve into the importance of making a good first impression, tips on how to introduce yourself confidently, and how to foster positive relationships with your classmates.

First impressions matter, and the way you introduce yourself sets the tone for how others perceive you. It is essential to be friendly, approachable, and authentic when meeting new people. Remember that everyone is in the same boat as you, trying to navigate the new school environment, so don't be afraid to take the first step in introducing yourself.

When introducing yourself to your new classmates, start by offering a warm smile and a friendly greeting. You can simply say, "Hi, my name is [your name], it's nice to meet you!" This simple gesture shows that you are open to making connections and sets a positive tone for the interaction. Remember to maintain eye contact and speak clearly and confidently to convey friendliness and approachability.

It's also a good idea to share a little bit about yourself when introducing yourself to classmates. You can mention where you are from, your interests, hobbies, or any fun facts about yourself. This helps to start a conversation and find common ground with your peers. For example, you could say, "I recently moved here from [previous location], and I love playing soccer and reading mystery novels."

Another important aspect of introducing yourself to classmates is being a good listener. After sharing a bit about yourself, show interest in learning about your classmates by asking questions and actively listening to their responses. This demonstrates that you are friendly, curious, and open to building new relationships.

To make the introduction process smoother, try to remember your classmates' names and use them when addressing them. This shows that you are attentive and respectful, which can help in building positive relationships with your peers. If you have trouble remembering names, you can try associating them with something unique about the person or repeating their name in conversation.

Lastly, don't be afraid to step out of your comfort zone and initiate conversations with different classmates. Making an effort to interact with a variety of people can help you expand your social circle and create a supportive network of friends.

In conclusion, introducing yourself to classmates is an important step in acclimating to a new school environment. By being friendly, approachable, and authentic, you can make a positive first impression and foster meaningful connections with your peers. Remember to be a good listener, share a bit about yourself, remember names, and initiate conversations to build strong relationships with your classmates. Embrace the opportunity to meet new people and form lasting friendships as you navigate your new school experience.

Being Open to New Experiences

Transitioning to a new school can be a mix of excitement and nervousness. One key attitude that can help ease the transition and make the most of your new school experience is being open to new experiences. Being open-minded means being willing to try new things, meet new people, and embrace the opportunities that come your way.

The night before your first day at your new school, take some time to reflect on the possibilities that lie ahead. Instead of focusing on any worries or uncertainties, remind yourself of the excitement of stepping into a new environment. Visualize yourself approaching the day with a positive attitude and an open mind, ready to embrace whatever comes your way.

As you navigate your way around the new school on your first day, remember that it's okay to feel a little lost or unsure. Being open to new experiences means being willing to ask for directions, seek help when needed, and approach each new encounter as a chance to learn and grow. Your new teacher and classmates are all potential sources of support and friendship, so don't hesitate to introduce yourself and start building connections.

One way to be open to new experiences is to participate in activities and events that may be different from what you're used to. Whether it's joining a club, trying out for a sports team, or engaging in a school project, stepping out of your comfort zone can lead to exciting discoveries and opportunities for personal growth. By saying "yes" to new experiences, you open yourself up to a world of possibilities and connections that can enrich your school experience.

Being open-minded also involves being flexible and adaptable to change. As you settle into your new school routine, be prepared for unexpected challenges and surprises. Instead of resisting change or feeling frustrated by disruptions, approach them with a mindset of curiosity and resilience. Embrace the unknown as a chance to learn more about yourself and your capabilities.

Another important aspect of being open to new experiences is being receptive to different perspectives and ideas. Your new school environment may be diverse in terms of cultural backgrounds, beliefs, and interests. Take this opportunity to engage with others who may have different viewpoints than your own. By listening and learning from others, you can broaden your understanding of the world and develop empathy and respect for different ways of thinking.

In conclusion, being open to new experiences is a mindset that can enhance your transition to a new school and enrich your overall learning journey. By approaching each day with a sense of curiosity, positivity, and a willingness to embrace the unknown, you can maximize the opportunities for growth, connection, and discovery that your new school has to offer. Remember, the key to thriving in a new environment is to keep an open heart and mind, ready to embrace the endless possibilities that come your way.

Chapter 5

Making New Friends

Smiling and Saying Hello

Making new friends can be an exciting yet daunting task, especially when starting at a new school. One of the simplest and most effective ways to initiate a connection with others is by smiling and saying hello. Your positive attitude and friendly demeanor can go a long way in building new relationships and creating a welcoming environment for yourself and those around you.

The Power of Smiling:

A smile is a universal gesture that transcends language barriers and cultural differences. It instantly conveys warmth, approachability, and friendliness. When you smile at someone, you are signaling openness and inviting them to engage with you. A smile is contagious and can create a ripple effect, brightening up someone else's day and setting a positive tone for your interactions.

Saying Hello:

Simple greetings like "hello" are the building blocks of communication and social interaction. By saying hello to your classmates, teachers, and other school staff, you are acknowledging their presence and showing respect. It demonstrates your willingness to connect and engage with others in a friendly manner. Remember that a genuine hello accompanied by a smile can make a significant difference in how you are perceived and how others respond to you.

Breaking the Ice:
Initiating conversations with new people can feel intimidating, but a smile and a hello can serve as an icebreaker. It provides a friendly opening that invites further interaction. When you approach someone with a smile and a hello, you are signaling that you are approachable and interested in getting to know them. This simple gesture can pave the way for meaningful conversations and the start of new friendships.

Creating a Positive Atmosphere:
By consistently smiling and saying hello to those around you, you contribute to creating a positive and inclusive atmosphere in your new school. Your friendly demeanor can help to alleviate any initial awkwardness or tension, making it easier for others to approach you and for you to feel more comfortable in your new environment. Remember that a welcoming smile and a friendly greeting can go a long way in fostering a sense of community and belonging.

Building Confidence:
Smiling and saying hello are not only ways to connect with others but also ways to build your own confidence and self-assurance. When you approach new situations with a positive attitude and a willingness to engage with others, you are demonstrating your social skills and ability to adapt to new environments. Each smile and hello you share can boost your own sense of self-esteem and make you feel more at ease in your new surroundings.

In conclusion, smiling and saying hello are powerful tools for making new friends and building a sense of community in your new school. These simple gestures can have a big impact on your social interactions, helping you to connect with others, break the ice, create a positive atmosphere, and build your own confidence. So, don't underestimate the power of a smile and a hello – they can be the first steps towards forming lasting friendships and enjoying a fulfilling school experience.

Joining Clubs and Activities

Joining clubs and activities at a new school can be an exciting and rewarding experience for students. It provides an opportunity to meet new people, learn new skills, and be a part of a community that shares your interests. In this chapter, we will explore the benefits of joining clubs and activities, how to find the right ones for you, and tips for making the most of your involvement.

Participating in clubs and activities can help you expand your social circle and make new friends. When you join a club or activity that aligns with your interests, you are likely to meet like-minded individuals who share your passion. This can make the transition to a new school easier as you already have something in common with your peers. Whether you enjoy sports, arts, music, or academics, there is a club or activity for everyone to get involved in.

Furthermore, joining clubs and activities can help you develop important skills that go beyond the classroom. For example, being part of a team can teach you about collaboration, communication, and leadership. Participating in a club that focuses on a specific skill or interest can also help you build expertise in that area. These experiences can enhance your personal growth and make you a well-rounded individual.

To find the right clubs and activities for you, consider your interests and passions. Think about what activities make you happy and what skills you would like to develop. Attend club fairs or information sessions at your new school to learn about the different options available. Talk to current students or teachers to get recommendations based on your interests.

Once you have identified the clubs and activities you want to join, take the initiative to get involved. Attend meetings regularly, participate in events, and engage with other members. Don't be afraid to step out of your comfort zone and try new things. Remember that joining clubs and activities is a great way to explore your interests and discover new talents.

When participating in clubs and activities, it's important to be respectful and open-minded towards others. Treat your fellow club members with kindness and be willing to listen to different perspectives. Collaboration and teamwork are key components of a successful club experience, so make an effort to contribute positively to the group dynamic.

Lastly, make the most of your club and activity involvement by setting goals for yourself. Whether it's improving a specific skill, taking on a leadership role, or making new friends, having clear objectives can help you stay motivated and engaged. Don't be afraid to challenge yourself and push your boundaries – growth often comes from stepping outside of your comfort zone.

In conclusion, joining clubs and activities at your new school can be a rewarding experience that enhances your social life, personal development, and academic journey. By exploring your interests, getting involved, and setting goals, you can make the most of your club experience and create lasting memories with your peers.

Finding Friends with Similar Interests

Finding friends with similar interests can be a rewarding and fulfilling experience when transitioning to a new school. Chapter 5 of the book "Book about Changing Schools" emphasizes the importance of building connections with peers who share common hobbies, passions, and activities. Establishing friendships based on shared interests can create a sense of belonging, foster mutual understanding, and provide a support system during the adjustment period.

One of the first steps in finding friends with similar interests is to observe and engage with your new school community. Pay attention to the clubs, sports teams, and extracurricular activities offered at your new school. Joining a club or participating in a team sport can be an excellent way to meet like-minded individuals who share your enthusiasm for a particular activity. Whether it's joining the art club, the chess team, or the drama club, engaging in shared interests can lead to meaningful connections with your peers.

Furthermore, don't hesitate to initiate conversations with classmates who exhibit interest in activities you enjoy. Making small talk about common hobbies or favorite pastimes can lead to discovering shared interests and potential friendships. By expressing your passion for a particular subject or activity, you may find others who resonate with your enthusiasm and are eager to connect over mutual interests.

Attending school events and social gatherings can also provide opportunities to meet individuals who share similar hobbies or passions. Whether it's a school dance, a sports game, or a talent show, participating in these events can facilitate interactions with peers who have common interests. Engaging in conversations with fellow students during these events can help you identify potential friends who share your hobbies and values.

In addition, don't be afraid to step outside of your comfort zone and try new activities or hobbies that interest you. Exploring different clubs, classes, or sports teams can introduce you to a diverse group of peers with varying interests. By being open-minded and willing to experiment with new experiences, you may discover new passions and forge connections with individuals who share your newfound interests.

It's essential to be genuine and authentic when building friendships based on shared interests. Be yourself and express your enthusiasm for the activities that bring you joy. Authenticity and sincerity can attract like-minded individuals who appreciate your genuine passion and authenticity.

In conclusion, finding friends with similar interests is a valuable aspect of navigating the social landscape of a new school. By actively seeking out peers who share your hobbies, passions, and activities, you can establish meaningful connections, cultivate a sense of belonging, and create a supportive network of friends who understand and appreciate your interests. Embrace the opportunity to connect with like-minded individuals, explore new activities, and foster friendships that enrich your school experience. Remember that friendships take time to develop, so be patient, open-minded, and proactive in building relationships with peers who share your interests.

Being Kind and Helpful

Being kind and helpful is a vital aspect of navigating the experience of changing schools. In Chapter 5 of the book "Book about Changing Schools," this topic is explored in depth to emphasize the importance of fostering positive relationships with peers in a new school setting.

One of the first steps in making new friends is to approach others with a friendly attitude. A simple smile and greeting can go a long way in initiating conversations and forming connections. By being open and approachable, you create a welcoming atmosphere that encourages others to interact with you.

Joining clubs and activities is another effective way to meet new people and establish common interests. By participating in extracurriculars, you have the opportunity to engage with like-minded individuals who share your passion for a particular hobby or subject. This shared interest serves as a foundation for building friendships based on mutual enjoyment and camaraderie.

When making new friends, it is essential to seek out individuals with whom you share common interests and values. By finding friends who align with your beliefs and preferences, you are more likely to form meaningful and lasting relationships. These connections can provide a sense of belonging and support as you navigate the challenges of adjusting to a new school environment.

Being kind and helpful towards others not only fosters positive relationships but also contributes to a supportive and inclusive school community. Acts of kindness, such as offering assistance to a classmate in need or including others in group activities, demonstrate empathy and compassion. By extending a helping hand to those around you, you create a culture of cooperation and goodwill that benefits everyone.

It is important to recognize that building friendships takes time and effort. Friendships are not formed overnight but require patience, understanding, and mutual respect. By investing in relationships and nurturing connections through shared experiences and conversations, you can cultivate meaningful bonds that enrich your social life and overall well-being.

In moments of uncertainty or doubt, it is crucial to communicate openly with your peers and seek support from trusted adults. Talking about your feelings and concerns can help alleviate stress and anxiety, while also strengthening your relationships with others. By expressing your thoughts and emotions, you invite understanding and empathy from those around you, fostering a sense of unity and solidarity within the school community.

Overall, being kind and helpful is a cornerstone of creating a positive and inclusive school environment. By approaching others with empathy, respect, and a willingness to connect, you not only forge meaningful friendships but also contribute to a culture of compassion and support. Embracing these values enhances your social interactions, promotes a sense of belonging, and enriches your overall school experience.

Understanding That Friendships Take Time

In the journey of changing schools, one of the key aspects that children may encounter is the process of making new friends. It is important for kids to understand that friendships take time to develop and that forming meaningful connections with others is a gradual process that requires patience and effort.

When transitioning to a new school, it is normal for children to feel eager to make friends quickly and to establish a sense of belonging in their new environment. However, it is essential to remind them that building strong friendships is not something that happens overnight. Just like any relationship, friendships require time, trust, and mutual respect to thrive.

One of the first steps in forming new friendships is to be open and approachable. Encouraging children to smile and say hello to their classmates is a simple yet effective way to start building connections. By showing kindness and a positive attitude, kids can create a welcoming atmosphere that makes it easier for others to approach them.

Joining clubs and activities is another great way for children to meet like-minded peers and develop common interests. Participating in extracurriculars not only provides opportunities to connect with others but also fosters a sense of community and teamwork. By engaging in activities they enjoy, kids are more likely to find friends who share their passions and values.

It is important for children to understand that making new friends is a gradual process that requires effort from both sides. Encouraging them to be kind, helpful, and considerate towards others can go a long way in building trust and forming lasting friendships. Teaching kids the value of empathy and understanding can help them navigate social situations with grace and compassion.

Friendships also take time to grow and evolve. Children should be reminded that relationships develop at their own pace, and it is normal to experience ups and downs along the way. Encouraging kids to communicate openly with their friends, share their thoughts and feelings, and resolve conflicts respectfully can strengthen their bonds and deepen their connections.

In times of uncertainty or doubt, children should know that it is okay to seek support from trusted adults. Whether it's a parent, teacher, or school counselor, having someone to talk to can provide guidance and reassurance during the process of making new friends. By fostering a supportive network of adults who care about their well-being, kids can feel more confident and secure as they navigate the challenges of building friendships.

Overall, understanding that friendships take time is a valuable lesson for children embarking on the journey of changing schools. By emphasizing patience, kindness, and communication, kids can cultivate meaningful relationships that enrich their lives and create a sense of belonging in their new school community. Encouraging them to embrace the journey of making new friends with an open heart and a positive attitude can lead to rewarding experiences and lasting connections that will stand the test of time.

Chapter 6

Dealing with Worries

Talking About Your Feelings

One of the most important aspects of transitioning to a new school is being able to talk about your feelings. Change can bring about a range of emotions, from excitement and anticipation to anxiety and sadness. It's essential to acknowledge and express these feelings in a healthy way to ensure a smooth adjustment to your new environment.

Talking about your feelings is a crucial step in coping with the challenges that come with changing schools. By opening up and sharing your emotions with trusted individuals, you can gain a better understanding of what you're going through and receive the support you need to navigate this transition successfully.

First and foremost, it's important to identify and recognize your emotions. Take the time to reflect on how you're feeling and why you might be feeling that way. Are you nervous about making new friends? Are you sad about leaving your old school behind? Are you excited about the opportunities that await you at your new school? By pinpointing your emotions, you can begin to address them more effectively.

Once you've identified your feelings, find someone you trust to talk to about them. This could be a parent, a teacher, a counselor, or a close friend. Expressing your emotions to someone who cares about you can provide you with a sense of relief and validation. They can offer perspective, empathy, and guidance to help you work through your feelings in a constructive manner.

When discussing your emotions, be honest and open about how you're feeling. Articulate your thoughts and concerns clearly, and don't be afraid to show vulnerability. It's essential to communicate your emotions authentically so that others can understand what you're going through and offer meaningful support.

Additionally, it's important to listen actively when talking about your feelings. Allow the person you're confiding in to provide feedback, advice, or simply a listening ear. By engaging in a two-way conversation, you can gain valuable insights and perspectives that may help you process your emotions more effectively.

Remember that it's normal to experience a range of emotions when facing significant changes like switching schools. It's okay to feel anxious, scared, or uncertain. By talking about your feelings, you can acknowledge and address these emotions in a healthy way, rather than bottling them up inside.

In conclusion, talking about your feelings is a vital part of adjusting to a new school. By recognizing, expressing, and discussing your emotions with trusted individuals, you can navigate the challenges of change more effectively. Remember that you're not alone in this journey, and there are people who care about you and are willing to support you through this transition. Embrace the opportunity to communicate openly about your feelings and take proactive steps towards a positive and fulfilling school experience.

Knowing That It's Normal to Be Nervous

Starting at a new school can be an exciting but nerve-wracking experience for many students. It's completely normal to feel anxious, worried, or nervous about the unknowns that come with transitioning to a different educational environment. In this chapter, we will explore why it's common to experience these feelings and provide strategies for managing and overcoming them.

First and foremost, it's important for students to understand that feeling nervous about starting at a new school is a natural response to change. Change can be challenging, as it often involves stepping out of your comfort zone and facing unfamiliar situations. It's okay to feel a mix of emotions, including excitement, fear, and uncertainty. Acknowledging these feelings and accepting them as part of the process can help alleviate some of the pressure associated with starting anew.

One of the main reasons why students may feel nervous about transitioning to a new school is the fear of the unknown. Not knowing what to expect in terms of academics, social dynamics, and school culture can be intimidating. To combat this uncertainty, it can be helpful for students to gather as much information as possible about their new school. This can include visiting the school prior to the first day, meeting with teachers and staff, and learning about the various programs and resources available. The more familiar students become with their new environment, the more confident and prepared they will feel.

Another common source of anxiety for students is the fear of not fitting in or making friends. Making new friends can be daunting, especially if you are entering a school where you don't know anyone. However, it's important to remember that many of your classmates are likely feeling the same way. By being open, approachable, and friendly, you can increase your chances of forming meaningful connections with others. Joining clubs, sports teams, or extracurricular activities can also be a great way to meet like-minded individuals and expand your social circle.

When feelings of nervousness arise, it's essential for students to have healthy coping mechanisms in place. Talking about your feelings with a trusted adult, such as a parent, teacher, or school counselor, can provide much-needed support and reassurance. These individuals can offer guidance, advice, and perspective on how to navigate the challenges of starting at a new school. Additionally, practicing relaxation techniques, such as deep breathing exercises or mindfulness meditation, can help calm the mind and reduce stress levels.

Finally, it's crucial for students to remind themselves that it's okay to make mistakes and take time to adjust to their new surroundings. Rome wasn't built in a day, and neither is a successful transition to a new school. Embracing the learning process, being patient with yourself, and staying positive can go a long way in overcoming nervousness and building confidence in your abilities.

In conclusion, feeling nervous about starting at a new school is a common experience shared by many students. By acknowledging and accepting these feelings, gathering information about your new school, making an effort to connect with others, seeking support when needed, and practicing self-care, you can successfully navigate the challenges of transitioning to a new educational environment. Remember, it's okay to be nervous – it's all part of the journey towards personal growth and development.

Asking Questions When You're Confused

In the process of transitioning to a new school, it is completely normal to feel confused or unsure about various aspects of your new environment. Whether it's understanding the class schedule, navigating the school campus, or grasping new concepts in your coursework, asking questions when you're confused is a crucial skill to develop. By seeking clarification and guidance when needed, you not only demonstrate a proactive approach to your learning but also pave the way for a smoother adjustment to your new school. In this chapter, we will delve into the importance of asking questions, how to effectively seek help, and the benefits of clarifying your doubts.

First and foremost, it is essential to recognize that everyone encounters moments of confusion or uncertainty, especially when faced with new challenges. Rather than feeling embarrassed or hesitant to ask questions, remind yourself that seeking clarification is a sign of maturity and a willingness to learn. By acknowledging your confusion and actively seeking solutions, you are taking control of your learning journey and demonstrating a growth mindset.

When you find yourself confused or unsure about a particular topic, don't hesitate to reach out to your teachers, classmates, or school counselors for assistance. Remember that educators are there to support you and are more than willing to help clarify any doubts you may have. Approach them with a positive attitude and a willingness to learn, and they will appreciate your proactive approach to seeking understanding.

When formulating your questions, be specific and concise to ensure that you receive the information you need. Instead of simply stating, "I don't understand this," try to pinpoint the exact aspect that is causing confusion. For example, you could ask, "Could you explain how to solve this math problem step by step?" or "Can you clarify the main points of this historical event?" By providing context to your questions, you enable others to offer targeted assistance that addresses your specific concerns.

Additionally, don't be afraid to ask follow-up questions if you require further clarification. Learning is a continuous process, and seeking additional information or examples can help solidify your understanding of the topic at hand. Engage in active listening during explanations and take notes if necessary to aid in your comprehension.

Asking questions when you're confused not only benefits your own learning but also fosters a sense of community and collaboration within your new school environment. By openly seeking help and guidance, you demonstrate a willingness to engage with others and create a supportive network of peers and mentors. Remember that everyone has different strengths and areas of expertise, so don't hesitate to leverage the knowledge and insights of those around you.

In conclusion, asking questions when you're confused is a fundamental aspect of navigating the challenges of a new school environment. By embracing a proactive approach to seeking clarification, you empower yourself to overcome obstacles, deepen your understanding, and forge meaningful connections with others. Remember that confusion is a natural part of the learning process, and by embracing it as an opportunity for growth, you set yourself on a path towards academic success and personal development.

Finding a Trusted Adult to Talk To

When transitioning to a new school, it is common to experience a range of emotions, uncertainties, and worries. During such times of change, having a trusted adult to talk to can make a significant difference in a child's ability to adapt and thrive in their new environment. Whether it's a parent, guardian, teacher, counselor, or family friend, having someone who can offer support, guidance, and a listening ear can help ease the transition process and provide comfort during challenging moments.

One of the key benefits of having a trusted adult to talk to is the opportunity to express feelings and concerns in a safe and non-judgmental space. Children may feel overwhelmed by the changes that come with switching schools, such as making new friends, adjusting to a different academic curriculum, or navigating unfamiliar social dynamics. By confiding in a trusted adult, children can openly share their thoughts, fears, and uncertainties, which can help them process their emotions and gain perspective on their situation.

Moreover, a trusted adult can offer valuable insights, advice, and reassurance to children facing new school transitions. Adults with experience and wisdom can provide guidance on how to approach challenges, cope with stress, and build resilience in the face of change. They can offer practical strategies for making new friends, managing academic demands, and adapting to a different school culture. By tapping into the wisdom of a trusted adult, children can gain valuable support and encouragement as they navigate the unfamiliar terrain of a new school.

In addition to providing emotional support and guidance, a trusted adult can serve as a role model for children as they adjust to a new school environment. By observing how adults handle challenges, communicate effectively, and demonstrate resilience, children can learn valuable life skills that can help them thrive in their new surroundings. Adults can model healthy coping mechanisms, effective problem-solving strategies, and positive attitudes towards change, which can inspire children to approach their own challenges with confidence and optimism.

Furthermore, having a trusted adult to talk to can help children build strong relationships and foster a sense of belonging in their new school community. By establishing a bond of trust and communication with an adult figure, children can feel supported, valued, and connected to their school environment. This sense of belonging can enhance children's self-esteem, motivation, and overall well-being, enabling them to navigate the ups and downs of the school transition with greater resilience and confidence.

In conclusion, finding a trusted adult to talk to is a crucial component of a successful school transition for children. By having a supportive and understanding adult figure in their corner, children can navigate the challenges of a new school environment with greater ease, resilience, and confidence. Whether seeking emotional support, practical advice, or simply a listening ear, having a trusted adult to turn to can make a world of difference in helping children adapt, grow, and thrive in their new academic setting.

Learning Relaxation Techniques

Learning relaxation techniques is an essential skill that can help children cope with the stress and anxiety that often accompany changing schools. In Chapter 6 of the 'Book about Changing Schools,' the focus is on providing practical strategies for managing worries and promoting emotional well-being. Let's delve into the detailed section about learning relaxation techniques.

Understanding the Importance of Relaxation Techniques

As children navigate the challenges of transitioning to a new school, they may experience a range of emotions such as nervousness, fear, and uncertainty. These emotions can manifest physically, leading to symptoms like tension headaches, stomachaches, or difficulty sleeping. Learning relaxation techniques is crucial as it offers children a way to calm their minds and bodies, reducing stress levels and promoting a sense of inner peace.

Practicing Deep Breathing

One of the simplest and most effective relaxation techniques is deep breathing. Encourage children to find a quiet and comfortable spot where they can sit or lie down. Instruct them to take slow, deep breaths in through their nose, hold for a few seconds, and then exhale slowly through their mouth. Deep breathing helps to slow down the heart rate, relax the muscles, and clear the mind of anxious thoughts.

Progressive Muscle Relaxation

Another valuable technique is progressive muscle relaxation. This involves systematically tensing and then relaxing different muscle groups in the body. Have children start by tightening their fists for a few seconds, then releasing and feeling the tension melt away. Guide them through each muscle group, from the toes to the head, focusing on the sensation of relaxation as they let go of tension.

Visualization and Guided Imagery

Visualization techniques can also be powerful tools for relaxation. Encourage children to close their eyes and imagine a peaceful scene, such as a tranquil beach or a serene forest. Guide them to engage their senses by picturing the sights, sounds, and smells of this imaginary place. This practice can transport them to a calming mental space and provide a welcome respite from worries.

Mindfulness and Meditation

Introducing children to mindfulness practices can help them cultivate a sense of awareness and presence in the moment. Teach them simple meditation techniques, such as focusing on their breath or repeating a calming phrase silently. By practicing mindfulness regularly, children can learn to observe their thoughts without judgment and develop greater emotional resilience.

Engaging in Relaxing Activities

Encourage children to explore different activities that promote relaxation, such as listening to soothing music, drawing or coloring, practicing yoga or gentle stretching, or spending time in nature. Engaging in activities that bring joy and peace can be a valuable way for children to unwind and recharge amidst the demands of adjusting to a new school environment.

In conclusion, learning relaxation techniques empowers children with valuable tools to manage stress and cultivate emotional well-being during the transition to a new school. By practicing deep breathing, progressive muscle relaxation, visualization, mindfulness, and engaging in relaxing activities, children can develop resilience, cope with worries, and nurture a sense of inner calm as they navigate the challenges of change.

Chapter 7

Staying Organized

Keeping Track of Homework and Projects

Keeping track of homework and projects is an essential skill for students transitioning to a new school. In Chapter 7 of the book "Book about Changing Schools," this topic is explored in depth to help students stay organized and on top of their academic responsibilities. Let's delve into the importance of keeping track of homework and projects and provide practical tips for students to succeed in this area.

One of the key reasons for keeping track of homework and projects is to ensure that students are completing their assignments on time and to the best of their ability. By staying organized and having a system in place to monitor their tasks, students can avoid last-minute cramming and reduce stress levels associated with looming deadlines.

Using a planner or calendar is a highly effective method for keeping track of homework and projects. Encouraging students to write down all their assignments, due dates, and important deadlines in one central location helps them visualize their workload and prioritize tasks accordingly. Whether it's a paper planner, a digital calendar, or a smartphone app, finding a method that works best for the student's individual preferences is crucial.

Setting up a homework routine is another key aspect of staying organized. Establishing a consistent study schedule that includes dedicated time for completing assignments, studying for tests, and reviewing class materials can help students develop good study habits and improve their time management skills. By creating a routine, students can better manage their workload and avoid procrastination.

It's important for students to ask for help when needed. If they are struggling with a particular assignment or concept, they should not hesitate to reach out to their teachers, classmates, or parents for assistance. Seeking help early on can prevent misunderstandings from snowballing into larger issues and can ultimately lead to a better understanding of the material.

Staying focused and motivated is essential when keeping track of homework and projects. Encouraging students to eliminate distractions, such as electronic devices or noise, while working on assignments can help them maintain their concentration and productivity. Setting small goals and rewarding themselves for completing tasks can also boost motivation and make the workload more manageable.

By staying organized, following a homework routine, seeking help when needed, and staying focused and motivated, students can effectively keep track of their homework and projects at their new school. These skills not only promote academic success but also instill valuable habits that can benefit students throughout their educational journey.

In conclusion, keeping track of homework and projects is a fundamental aspect of a student's academic success. By implementing practical strategies and staying organized, students can navigate the challenges of transitioning to a new school with confidence and resilience. By developing strong organizational skills and effective study habits, students can excel academically and thrive in their new school environment.

Using a Planner or Calendar

Using a planner or calendar is an essential skill for students changing schools as it helps them stay organized, manage their time effectively, and reduce stress. In Chapter 7 of the book "Book about Changing Schools," the focus is on the importance of staying organized and how using a planner or calendar can aid in this process.

The Importance of Using a Planner or Calendar

Transitioning to a new school can be overwhelming, with new schedules, assignments, and activities to keep track of. Using a planner or calendar can help students stay on top of their responsibilities and avoid feeling overwhelmed. By writing down important dates, deadlines, and tasks, students can better manage their time and prioritize their commitments.

Benefits of Using a Planner or Calendar

1. Time Management: A planner or calendar allows students to schedule their time effectively, ensuring they allocate enough time for studying, completing assignments, attending extracurricular activities, and maintaining a healthy balance between school and personal life.

2. Organization: By having a central place to record all important dates and tasks, students can avoid missing deadlines or forgetting important events. This can help reduce stress and improve productivity.

3. Prioritization: With a planner or calendar, students can prioritize their tasks based on deadlines and importance. This helps them focus on what needs to be done first and avoid procrastination.

4. Tracking Progress: Using a planner or calendar allows students to track their progress on assignments, projects, and goals. This can provide a sense of accomplishment and motivation to keep working towards their objectives.

Tips for Using a Planner or Calendar Effectively

1. Choose the Right Format: Students can opt for a physical planner or an electronic calendar based on their preferences. Some may prefer the tangible aspect of writing things down, while others may find digital tools more convenient for access and reminders.

2. Regular Updates: Make it a habit to update the planner or calendar regularly. This includes adding new assignments, events, and deadlines as they come up, as well as reviewing and adjusting your schedule as needed.

3. Color-Coding: Using different colors for different types of tasks can help visually organize the information in the planner or calendar. For example, using one color for homework assignments, another for extracurricular activities, and so on.

4. Set Reminders: Utilize reminder features in electronic calendars or set alarms for important deadlines. This can help ensure that tasks are not forgotten and are completed on time.

5. Review Daily: Take a few minutes each day to review your planner or calendar. This can help you stay on top of your tasks, make adjustments as needed, and prepare for upcoming events.

By incorporating the use of a planner or calendar into their daily routine, students changing schools can enhance their organizational skills, improve time management, and reduce stress. This valuable tool can support them in navigating the challenges of transitioning to a new school and help them achieve academic and personal success.

Setting Up a Homework Routine

Setting up a homework routine is essential for students transitioning to a new school. A structured routine can help students stay organized, manage their time effectively, and ultimately succeed academically. In this chapter, we will discuss the importance of establishing a homework routine, provide tips on how to create an effective schedule, and offer strategies to stay on track.

Importance of a Homework Routine

Homework plays a crucial role in reinforcing classroom learning, developing independent study skills, and preparing students for exams. By establishing a homework routine, students can create a dedicated time and space for completing assignments, studying for tests, and reviewing class materials. A consistent routine can also help reduce procrastination, improve time management skills, and alleviate stress associated with academic responsibilities.

Creating an Effective Schedule

To create an effective homework routine, students should first assess their workload, understand their learning preferences, and identify the best time of day for studying. It is important to choose a quiet and well-lit study area free from distractions, such as electronic devices or noisy surroundings. Students should allocate specific blocks of time for different subjects or assignments and prioritize tasks based on deadlines or level of difficulty.

Tips for Staying on Track

Staying on track with a homework routine requires discipline, focus, and consistency. Here are some tips to help students maintain a successful study schedule:

1. Set specific goals: Break down assignments into manageable tasks and set achievable goals for each study session. This will help students stay motivated and track their progress.

2. Use a planner or calendar: Keep track of homework assignments, project deadlines, and test dates in a planner or digital calendar. This will help students plan ahead, avoid last-minute cramming, and manage their time effectively.

3. Establish a routine: Designate a regular time each day for studying and completing homework. Consistency is key to forming a habit, and having a set schedule can help students stay organized and focused.

4. Take breaks: To prevent burnout and maintain productivity, it is important to incorporate short breaks into study sessions. Stretching, walking, or grabbing a healthy snack can help refresh the mind and increase concentration.

5. Seek help when needed: If students encounter difficulties with assignments or concepts, they should not hesitate to ask for help from teachers, peers, or tutors. Seeking assistance can clarify doubts, improve understanding, and enhance learning outcomes.

By following these tips and strategies, students can establish a productive homework routine that supports their academic success and overall well-being. Consistency, organization, and perseverance are key to mastering time management skills and achieving academic goals in a new school environment.

Asking for Help When Needed

Transitioning to a new school can be a daunting experience, filled with unfamiliar faces, routines, and expectations. It is natural to feel overwhelmed or uncertain at times, and in such moments, knowing how and when to ask for help can make a significant difference in one's ability to navigate the new environment successfully.

The first step in asking for help is acknowledging that it is okay not to have all the answers. Everyone encounters moments of confusion or difficulty, and seeking assistance is a proactive way to address challenges and gain clarity. By recognizing the need for support, students demonstrate maturity and a willingness to learn and grow in their new school setting.

One effective strategy for asking for help is to identify trusted adults within the school community who are approachable and understanding. Whether it is a teacher, counselor, or school staff member, having a designated person to turn to can provide a sense of security and reassurance. These individuals are trained to assist students in various situations and can offer valuable guidance and support tailored to the student's needs.

When seeking help, it is important to communicate clearly and honestly about the specific issue or concern at hand. By articulating one's challenges or questions openly, students allow others to provide targeted assistance and solutions. Whether it is clarifying a classroom assignment, addressing a social issue, or seeking advice on managing stress, being transparent about one's needs enables others to offer relevant support.

Furthermore, asking for help is an active process that involves engaging in dialogue and collaboration with others. Students are encouraged to ask questions, seek clarification, and participate in problem-solving discussions to actively address their concerns. By taking an assertive approach to seeking help, students demonstrate initiative and a commitment to their own personal and academic growth.

In addition to seeking help from adults, students are also encouraged to reach out to their peers for support and guidance. Building positive relationships with classmates can create a sense of community and camaraderie that fosters mutual assistance and collaboration. Whether it is studying together, sharing insights, or offering encouragement, peer support can be a valuable resource in navigating the challenges of a new school environment.

Overall, the section on Asking for Help When Needed underscores the importance of proactive communication, seeking support from trusted individuals, and fostering a sense of community within the school environment. By embracing the willingness to ask for help, students empower themselves to overcome obstacles, build resilience, and thrive in their new school experience.

Staying Focused and Motivated

Staying focused and motivated during a transition to a new school can be challenging, but it is essential for a successful adjustment. In this chapter, we will explore strategies and techniques to help students maintain their focus and motivation throughout this period of change.

One of the first steps in staying focused and motivated is to establish a routine. Having a consistent schedule can provide structure and stability during a time of upheaval. Set aside specific times for homework, studying, extracurricular activities, and relaxation. By creating a routine, you can better manage your time and responsibilities, which can help reduce stress and improve productivity.

Another key aspect of staying focused and motivated is setting goals. Establish both short-term and long-term goals related to your academic performance, social relationships, and personal growth. By having clear objectives to work towards, you can stay motivated and focused on the tasks at hand. Make sure your goals are realistic, measurable, and achievable, and track your progress regularly to stay on track.

It's important to stay organized to maintain focus and motivation. Keep track of assignments, projects, and deadlines by using a planner or calendar. Break down larger tasks into smaller, manageable steps to prevent feeling overwhelmed. Stay on top of your responsibilities by prioritizing tasks and tackling them one at a time. If you find yourself struggling with a particular subject or assignment, don't hesitate to ask for help from your teachers, classmates, or parents.

Maintaining a positive attitude is crucial for staying motivated during a period of change. Focus on the opportunities and possibilities that come with a new school experience rather than dwelling on the challenges. Remind yourself of your strengths and capabilities, and believe in your ability to succeed in your new environment. Surround yourself with positive influences, whether it's supportive friends, family members, or teachers, who can encourage and motivate you along the way.

In addition to staying positive, taking care of your physical and mental well-being is essential for maintaining focus and motivation. Make sure to get enough sleep, eat well, and stay active to keep your energy levels up. Practice relaxation techniques such as deep breathing, mindfulness, or meditation to reduce stress and anxiety. Don't hesitate to talk to a trusted adult or counselor if you're feeling overwhelmed or struggling with your emotions.

Lastly, celebrate your successes and progress along the way. Acknowledge your achievements, no matter how small, and reward yourself for reaching milestones and goals. Reflect on how far you've come and the obstacles you've overcome to remind yourself of your resilience and determination. By recognizing and celebrating your accomplishments, you can stay motivated and inspired to continue pushing yourself to reach new heights.

In conclusion, staying focused and motivated during a transition to a new school requires effort, persistence, and a positive mindset. By establishing a routine, setting goals, staying organized, maintaining a positive attitude, taking care of your well-being, and celebrating your successes, you can navigate this period of change with confidence and resilience. Remember that change can be an opportunity for growth and self-discovery, and by staying focused and motivated, you can make the most of your new school experience.

Chapter 8

Staying Connected with Old Friends

Writing Letters or Emails

Writing letters or emails is a wonderful way to stay connected with old friends when transitioning to a new school. In Chapter 8 of the 'Book about Changing Schools,' this section highlights the importance and benefits of maintaining communication with friends from your previous school. Let's delve deeper into how writing letters or emails can help foster friendships and create lasting connections during this period of change.

When you move to a new school, it's completely normal to miss your old friends and the memories you shared together. Writing letters or emails is a thoughtful and personal way to keep in touch with them. It allows you to express your feelings, share updates about your new school experience, and reminisce about the good times you had together. By putting your thoughts into writing, you can communicate on a deeper level and bridge the physical distance between you and your friends.

One of the advantages of writing letters or emails is the ability to maintain a sense of continuity in your friendships. Even though you may not see each other every day like before, exchanging letters or emails keeps the connection alive. It provides a platform for ongoing communication, where you can share your thoughts, feelings, and experiences with your friends, creating a sense of closeness despite the distance.

Moreover, writing letters or emails allows you to practice and enhance your communication skills. As you articulate your thoughts and feelings in writing, you develop your ability to express yourself clearly and effectively. This skill is valuable not only for maintaining friendships but also for future endeavors such as academics and professional relationships. By engaging in regular correspondence with your friends, you nurture your communication skills in a meaningful and engaging way.

Another benefit of writing letters or emails is the opportunity to reflect and reminisce about shared experiences. As you exchange stories and updates with your friends, you create a virtual space where you can relive cherished memories and celebrate your friendship. Sharing anecdotes, inside jokes, and important milestones through letters or emails strengthens the bond you have with your friends and reinforces the connection you share.

Furthermore, writing letters or emails can serve as a source of comfort and support during the transition to a new school. Knowing that you have friends who care about you and are eager to hear from you can provide emotional reassurance and stability during times of change. Receiving a heartfelt letter or email from a friend can brighten your day, lift your spirits, and remind you that you are not alone in this journey.

In conclusion, writing letters or emails is a meaningful and effective way to stay connected with old friends when changing schools. It nurtures friendships, enhances communication skills, fosters a sense of continuity, encourages reflection, and provides emotional support during transitions. By embracing this form of communication, you can strengthen your relationships, maintain a sense of belonging, and create lasting connections that transcend physical distance.

Video Calls and Phone Chats

Video calls and phone chats play a crucial role in staying connected with old friends when transitioning to a new school. In Chapter 8 of the 'Book about Changing Schools,' this section emphasizes the importance of maintaining relationships with friends from your previous school through technology. It provides valuable insights and tips on how to effectively use video calls and phone chats to nurture friendships despite the physical distance.

One of the key benefits of video calls and phone chats is the ability to see and hear your friends in real-time, which helps bridge the gap created by the move to a new school. Through video calls, you can maintain a sense of closeness and intimacy that may be lacking in written communication. Seeing your friends' facial expressions and hearing their voices can make conversations more personal and meaningful, reinforcing the bond you share.

Moreover, video calls and phone chats offer a convenient way to catch up with old friends and share updates about your new school experience. By scheduling regular calls or chats, you can stay connected with your friends and continue to be a part of each other's lives, despite being physically apart. Sharing stories, experiences, and laughter through video calls can help you feel connected and supported during the transition period.

To make the most of video calls and phone chats, it is essential to establish a communication routine with your friends. Setting a regular time for calls or chats can create a sense of predictability and consistency in your interactions, making it easier to stay connected despite busy schedules. Additionally, being proactive in reaching out to your friends and initiating conversations shows that you value and prioritize your friendships, fostering a sense of mutual care and support.

In addition to maintaining existing friendships, video calls and phone chats can also be a great way to introduce your old friends to your new school environment. By giving them a virtual tour of your new school, introducing them to your classmates or teachers, and sharing your daily experiences through video calls, you can involve them in your transition process and make them feel like a part of your new school community.

Furthermore, video calls and phone chats provide a platform for emotional support and reassurance during moments of homesickness or adjustment challenges. Being able to talk to familiar faces and hear familiar voices can provide comfort and encouragement, helping you navigate the ups and downs of transitioning to a new school with greater resilience and confidence.

In conclusion, video calls and phone chats are invaluable tools for staying connected with old friends when changing schools. By embracing technology and making an effort to maintain communication with your friends, you can preserve and strengthen your relationships, even as you embark on a new chapter in your educational journey. Remember, distance may separate you physically, but with video calls and phone chats, your friendships can continue to thrive and grow despite the miles between you.

Planning Visits During Holidays

As a student transitioning to a new school, maintaining connections with old friends is crucial for a smooth adjustment. One way to nurture these relationships is through planning visits during holidays. These reunions can be a source of comfort and joy, helping you feel connected to your past while embracing your present circumstances.

When planning visits during holidays, it is essential to consider logistics and communication. Reach out to your old friends well in advance to discuss potential dates and activities. By coordinating schedules early on, you can ensure that everyone is available and excited for the reunion. Additionally, involve your parents in the planning process to address any transportation or accommodation needs.

During the visit, prioritize quality time spent together. Whether you choose to explore familiar hangout spots, reminisce about shared memories, or engage in new adventures, the key is to focus on building new experiences that strengthen your bond. Engaging in activities that you used to enjoy together can reignite the closeness you once shared and create lasting memories.

Moreover, be open to sharing your new school experiences with your old friends. Discussing your challenges and triumphs can deepen your connection by allowing them to understand your current journey. Similarly, listen attentively to their stories and struggles, showing empathy and support as they navigate their own paths.

In addition to personal interactions, technology can also play a valuable role in staying connected during holidays. Schedule regular video calls or phone chats with your friends, providing a sense of continuity in your relationships. Sharing updates and stories through messages or social media platforms can bridge the physical distance between you and maintain a sense of closeness.

Furthermore, when planning visits during holidays, consider involving your old friends in your new school life. Invite them to school events or performances, allowing them to witness your growth and achievements firsthand. By incorporating them into your present environment, you can create a seamless transition between your past and present social circles.

As you navigate these visits, it is essential to balance your time and attention between old and new friendships. While reconnecting with old friends is valuable, it is equally important to invest in building relationships at your new school. Striking this balance can enrich your social life and provide you with a diverse support network.

Finally, approach these reunions with a positive and open mindset. Embrace the opportunity to reconnect with familiar faces and cherish the bonds you have cultivated over time. By planning visits during holidays, you can reinforce the foundations of your friendships and create lasting connections that transcend physical distance.

In conclusion, planning visits during holidays is a meaningful way to stay connected with old friends while embarking on a new school journey. By prioritizing communication, quality time together, and a positive outlook, you can strengthen your relationships and navigate the transition with grace and resilience. Embrace these reunions as opportunities for growth, reflection, and shared experiences that contribute to your overall well-being and sense of belonging.

Sharing Updates and Stories

Moving to a new school can be an exciting but challenging experience, and maintaining relationships with friends from your previous school can provide a sense of comfort and continuity during this transition period. By sharing updates and stories with your old friends, you can keep them informed about your new school life and continue to nurture those important friendships.

One of the ways to stay connected with old friends is through writing letters or emails. Taking the time to sit down and craft a thoughtful message to your friends can help bridge the physical distance between you. Share with them your experiences at your new school, the new friends you have made, and any exciting events or activities you have been a part of. Receiving a letter or email from you will not only keep your friends updated but also show them that you value and care about your friendship.

Another effective way to stay connected with old friends is through video calls and phone chats. Thanks to technology, you can now have face-to-face conversations with your friends even if you are miles apart. Schedule regular video calls or phone chats with your friends to catch up on each other's lives, share funny anecdotes, and reminisce about the good times you had together. Seeing their faces and hearing their voices can help maintain the strong bond you share with your old friends.

Planning visits during holidays is another great way to stay connected with old friends. If possible, try to arrange a get-together during school breaks or holidays when you can reunite with your friends in person. Spend quality time together, create new memories, and cherish the moments you have with each other. These reunions can strengthen your friendship and provide a sense of belonging and familiarity amidst the changes in your life.

Sharing updates and stories with your old friends is not only about keeping them informed about your life but also about listening to their stories and experiences. Make sure to ask them about their new school, friends, and activities as well. By showing genuine interest in their lives, you demonstrate that your friendship is a two-way street built on mutual care and support.

Balancing old and new friendships is essential as you navigate the transition to a new school. While it's important to stay connected with your old friends, don't forget to invest time and effort in building new relationships at your new school. Each friendship brings its own unique value and contributes to your personal growth and development.

In conclusion, sharing updates and stories with old friends is a vital aspect of staying connected during the school transition process. By maintaining communication, showing care and interest, and balancing old and new friendships, you can navigate the changes in your life with a sense of continuity and support from those who know you best. Remember, friendships are a source of strength and joy, no matter the distance or circumstances.

Balancing Old and New Friendships

One of the most challenging aspects of changing schools is navigating the balance between maintaining old friendships while also forming new connections. It is natural to feel torn between the familiar comfort of old friends and the excitement of meeting new people. However, with the right approach and mindset, it is possible to successfully manage both old and new friendships during this transitional period.

First and foremost, it is essential to communicate openly and honestly with your old friends about your feelings and fears regarding the change. Let them know that even though you are starting a new chapter in your life, your bond with them remains important to you. By maintaining regular contact through phone calls, video chats, or letters, you can keep the connection alive despite the physical distance. Make an effort to share updates about your new school experiences while also listening to their stories and supporting them in their endeavors.

At the same time, it is crucial to embrace the opportunity to forge new friendships at your new school. Be open-minded and approachable, smile, and say hello to your classmates. Join clubs and activities that align with your interests to meet like-minded individuals who share your passions. Building new friendships takes time and effort, so be patient and allow relationships to develop naturally. Remember that everyone is in the same boat, looking to make connections and find their place in the new school environment.

Finding a balance between old and new friendships requires time management and prioritization. Allocate time for both sets of friends in your schedule, whether it's through regular communication with old friends or participating in activities with new friends. Keep in mind that it is okay to have different levels of closeness with various friends and that relationships evolve over time. Be present and engaged in your interactions, showing genuine interest and empathy towards others.

It is also important to maintain boundaries and set realistic expectations for both old and new friendships. Understand that it is normal for relationships to change as you grow and evolve, and not all friendships will withstand the test of time. Focus on cultivating meaningful connections that bring positivity and support into your life, whether they are old or new relationships. Be willing to let go of toxic or one-sided friendships and invest in those that uplift and inspire you.

In conclusion, balancing old and new friendships during a school transition is a delicate dance that requires patience, communication, and a positive attitude. Embrace the opportunity to broaden your social circle and learn from different perspectives while cherishing the bonds you have with old friends. Remember that friendships enrich our lives and contribute to our overall well-being, so nurture these connections with care and authenticity. By striking a harmonious balance between old and new friendships, you can navigate the challenges of changing schools with resilience and grace.

Chapter 9

Embracing the New School Experience

Exploring New Subjects and Activities

Exploring New Subjects and Activities is a pivotal part of the transition to a new school. It allows students to broaden their horizons, discover new passions, and make the most of their academic experience. In this chapter, we will delve into the importance of exploring new subjects and activities, as well as provide tips on how to navigate this exciting aspect of changing schools.

When transitioning to a new school, one of the most exciting opportunities is the chance to explore new subjects and activities. Whether it's a different curriculum, extracurricular programs, or unique electives, each new school offers a fresh perspective on learning. By embracing these opportunities, students can expand their knowledge, develop new skills, and discover hidden talents they may not have known they had.

One of the key benefits of exploring new subjects and activities is the ability to broaden one's horizons. Each subject offers a unique perspective on the world, allowing students to gain a deeper understanding of various topics. By taking the initiative to explore different subjects, students can discover new interests and passions that may shape their academic and career goals in the future.

Furthermore, participating in new activities can help students develop a well-rounded skill set. Whether it's joining a sports team, theater group, or academic club, extracurricular activities provide opportunities for students to hone their talents, build teamwork skills, and develop leadership qualities. These experiences not only enhance their academic performance but also contribute to their personal growth and development.

To make the most of exploring new subjects and activities, it's important for students to approach this process with an open mind and a willingness to step out of their comfort zone. Trying new things can be intimidating, but it's also incredibly rewarding. By taking risks and trying new activities, students can discover their strengths, overcome challenges, and build confidence in their abilities.

Here are some practical tips for students to navigate the process of exploring new subjects and activities:

1. Research the available options: Take the time to learn about the different subjects and activities offered at your new school. Talk to teachers, counselors, and fellow students to get a sense of what's available and what might interest you.

2. Attend information sessions: Many schools host orientation sessions or club fairs to introduce students to the various extracurricular opportunities available. Attend these events to learn more about the clubs, sports teams, and other activities you can participate in.

3. Try something new: Don't be afraid to step out of your comfort zone and try a subject or activity you've never considered before. You never know what you might discover about yourself and your interests.

4. Set goals: Whether it's mastering a new skill, making new friends, or simply having fun, set specific goals for your exploration of new subjects and activities. Having clear objectives can help you stay motivated and focused on your learning journey.

5. Stay committed: Once you've chosen a subject or activity to explore, give it your full commitment and dedication. Attend practices, participate in discussions, and engage with your peers to make the most of the experience.

In conclusion, exploring new subjects and activities is an essential part of the school transition process. By embracing new opportunities, students can expand their horizons, develop valuable skills, and discover their passions. With an open mind and a willingness to try new things, students can make the most of their academic experience and set themselves up for success in the future.

Finding What Makes Your New School Special

Transitioning to a new school can be a daunting experience for students. However, it can also be an exciting opportunity to discover what makes this new environment unique and special. In this chapter, we will explore ways to embrace the new school experience and find the aspects that make your new school stand out.

1. Exploring New Subjects and Activities:
One of the first steps in finding what makes your new school special is to explore the different subjects and activities that are offered. Take the time to attend various classes, clubs, and extracurricular activities to see what interests you. You may discover new passions or talents that you never knew you had. Embrace the opportunity to learn and grow in these areas, as they can shape your overall school experience.

2. Getting Involved in School Events:
Participating in school events is a great way to immerse yourself in the culture and community of your new school. Whether it's a sports game, a talent show, or a fundraising event, getting involved shows your school spirit and allows you to connect with your peers and teachers outside of the classroom. By being an active participant in these events, you can create lasting memories and build a sense of belonging within the school community.

3. Setting New Goals and Challenges:
Setting goals and challenges for yourself can help you stay motivated and focused in your new school environment. Whether it's aiming for a certain grade point average, joining a new club, or trying out for a sports team, having goals gives you a sense of purpose and direction. Embrace these challenges as opportunities for personal growth and development, and celebrate your achievements along the way.

4. Celebrating Your Progress and Success:
As you navigate your new school experience, it's important to acknowledge and celebrate your progress and success. Whether it's acing a difficult test, making new friends, or mastering a new

skill, take the time to pat yourself on the back and recognize your accomplishments. By celebrating your successes, you build confidence and resilience that will carry you through future challenges.

5. Finding What Makes Your New School Special:
Every school has its own unique qualities and characteristics that make it special. It could be a supportive and inclusive community, a strong emphasis on creativity and innovation, or a wide range of resources and opportunities for students. Take the time to discover what sets your new school apart from others and embrace these qualities. Whether it's the dedicated teachers, the vibrant school spirit, or the diverse student body, finding what makes your new school special can help you feel connected and engaged in your educational journey.

In conclusion, finding what makes your new school special is a process of exploration, involvement, goal-setting, and celebration. Embrace the opportunities that come with a new school experience, and remember that each day is a chance to discover something new and exciting about your school environment. By staying open-minded and proactive, you can create a fulfilling and meaningful experience at your new school.

Getting Involved in School Events

Getting involved in school events is a great way for students to immerse themselves in the school community, make new friends, and create lasting memories. In Chapter 9 of the book 'Book about Changing Schools,' the focus shifts to embracing the new school experience by actively participating in various school events and activities.

School events come in all shapes and sizes, from academic competitions to sports games, talent shows to community service projects. By participating in these events, students can not only showcase their talents and skills but also develop important social and teamwork skills that will benefit them both in and out of the classroom.

One of the first steps in getting involved in school events is to keep an eye out for upcoming opportunities. Schools often have a calendar of events that students can refer to, listing everything from club meetings to school plays to fundraising events. By staying informed about what's happening at school, students can choose events that align with their interests and availability.

Once students have identified events they want to participate in, it's important to take the initiative to sign up or volunteer. Whether it's joining a sports team, auditioning for a school play, or helping to organize a charity event, getting involved requires a proactive approach. By putting themselves out there and getting involved, students can make meaningful connections with their peers and teachers, and feel a sense of ownership and pride in their school community.

Participating in school events also provides students with opportunities to develop important life skills. For example, being part of a team or committee teaches students how to collaborate, communicate effectively, and problem-solve collectively. These skills are not only valuable in school but also in future endeavors such as college and careers.

Moreover, involvement in school events can boost students' confidence and self-esteem. By stepping outside their comfort zones and trying new things, students can discover hidden talents and strengths they never knew they had. Whether it's giving a speech at a school assembly or leading a group project, participating in school events allows students to showcase their abilities and be recognized for their contributions.

Additionally, school events provide a break from the routine of everyday academics and offer a chance for students to have fun and relax. Whether it's attending a school dance, cheering on the school's sports teams, or participating in a talent show, school events offer students a chance to socialize, have fun, and create positive memories that will last a lifetime.

In conclusion, getting involved in school events is a valuable aspect of the school experience that offers numerous benefits to students. From developing important life skills to boosting confidence and creating lasting memories, participating in school events can enrich students' educational journey and foster a sense of belonging and community within the school. By actively engaging in school events, students can make the most of their time at school and create a fulfilling and rewarding experience.

Setting New Goals and Challenges

As you navigate the exciting and sometimes challenging experience of changing schools, setting new goals and challenges can help you thrive in your new environment and continue to grow as a student and individual. In this chapter, we will explore the importance of setting goals, how to identify meaningful challenges, and strategies for staying motivated and focused on your aspirations.

Setting new goals is a powerful way to channel your energy and focus in a positive direction. When you change schools, you have a unique opportunity to redefine your academic and personal objectives. Take some time to reflect on what you hope to achieve in your new school and what areas you would like to improve upon. Whether it's excelling in a particular subject, making new friends, or getting involved in extracurricular activities, setting specific, measurable goals can help you stay motivated and track your progress.

When setting goals, it's important to make them realistic and achievable. Start by identifying short-term goals that you can work towards in the near future, such as improving your grades in a challenging subject or joining a new club. Additionally, consider setting long-term goals that align with your overall aspirations, such as pursuing leadership roles in school organizations or preparing for college applications.

Challenges are another essential component of personal growth and development. By embracing challenges, you can push yourself out of your comfort zone, build resilience, and discover your potential. When selecting challenges to pursue, consider your interests, strengths, and areas for growth. Whether it's participating in a public speaking competition, taking on a leadership role in a club, or tackling a difficult academic project, challenges can provide valuable learning experiences and opportunities for personal achievement.

To effectively tackle new challenges, it's important to approach them with a positive mindset and a willingness to learn from setbacks. Embrace the process of growth and improvement, even when faced with obstacles or setbacks. Seek support from teachers, mentors, or peers when needed, and don't be afraid to ask for help or guidance along the way. Remember that challenges are opportunities for learning and growth, and each experience, whether successful or not, can contribute to your personal development.

Staying motivated and focused on your goals and challenges can be challenging at times, especially in a new school environment. To maintain your enthusiasm and drive, create a plan of action with specific steps to achieve your objectives. Break down your goals into manageable tasks, set deadlines for completion, and celebrate your achievements along the way. Stay organized, prioritize your commitments, and stay committed to your aspirations, even when faced with distractions or obstacles.

In conclusion, setting new goals and challenges can empower you to thrive in your new school environment and continue your journey of personal growth and development. By identifying meaningful objectives, embracing challenges, and staying motivated and focused, you can make the most of your school experience and discover your strengths, passions, and potential. Embrace the opportunities for growth and learning that come with change, and remember that each goal achieved and challenge overcome brings you one step closer to realizing your full potential.

Celebrating Your Progress and Success

As you navigate the challenges and triumphs of transitioning to a new school, it is important to take a moment to pause and reflect on your journey. Celebrating your progress and success is a vital part of acknowledging your hard work and perseverance throughout this transformative experience.

One way to celebrate your progress is to set small, achievable goals for yourself. These goals could be academic, social, or personal in nature. By setting goals and working towards them, you can track your progress and celebrate each milestone you reach. Whether it's improving your grades in a challenging subject, making new friends, or simply feeling more confident in your new school environment, each step forward is worthy of celebration.

Another way to celebrate your progress is to acknowledge your strengths and accomplishments. Take note of the skills you have developed, the obstacles you have overcome, and the personal growth you have experienced since starting at your new school. Recognize the resilience and adaptability you have demonstrated throughout this transition and give yourself credit for your efforts.

Celebrating your success can also involve sharing your achievements with others. Whether it's your parents, teachers, friends, or classmates, don't be shy about sharing your accomplishments and milestones. By sharing your successes with others, you not only reinforce your own sense of achievement but also inspire and motivate those around you.

It's important to remember that celebrating your progress and success is not just about external validation or recognition. It's also about honoring your own journey and acknowledging the hard work and dedication you have put into adapting to your new school environment. Take time to reflect on the challenges you have faced, the lessons you have learned, and the growth you have experienced along the way.

As you celebrate your progress and success, don't forget to practice self-care and self-compassion. Treat yourself kindly and indulge in activities that bring you joy and relaxation. Whether it's spending time with loved ones, engaging in a favorite hobby, or simply taking a moment to appreciate how far you have come, self-care is an essential part of celebrating your achievements.

Lastly, remember that celebrating your progress and success is an ongoing process. As you continue to navigate the ups and downs of your new school experience, take time to pause and acknowledge the strides you have made. By celebrating your progress along the way, you can stay motivated, build resilience, and cultivate a positive attitude towards change and growth.

In conclusion, celebrating your progress and success is a meaningful way to honor your journey, recognize your achievements, and foster a sense of pride and accomplishment. By setting goals, acknowledging your strengths, sharing your successes, practicing self-care, and maintaining a positive attitude, you can celebrate your progress and success in a way that is meaningful and fulfilling.

Chapter 10

Looking Back and Moving Forward

Reflecting on Your Journey

As you near the end of your journey of changing schools, it's important to take a moment to reflect on the experiences you've had and the growth you've undergone. Reflecting on your journey can provide valuable insights, help you appreciate how far you've come, and prepare you for the next chapter in your life.

1. Acknowledging Your Accomplishments: Take a moment to acknowledge and celebrate the accomplishments you've achieved since changing schools. Whether it's making new friends, excelling in a particular subject, or overcoming a challenge, recognizing your achievements can boost your confidence and self-esteem.

2. Identifying Challenges and Lessons Learned: Reflect on the challenges you faced during the transition to a new school. Consider what you've learned from these challenges and how they have helped you grow as a person. Every obstacle you've overcome has contributed to your resilience and strength.

3. Recognizing Personal Growth: Think about how you have grown and changed since starting at your new school. Have you become more confident, independent, or adaptable? Reflect on the personal growth you've experienced and how it has shaped you into the person you are today.

4. Gratitude and Appreciation: Take time to express gratitude for the people who have supported you throughout this journey. Whether it's your family, friends, teachers, or mentors, acknowledge their role in helping you navigate the changes and challenges of changing schools. Expressing gratitude can foster stronger relationships and a sense of connection.

5. Setting New Goals: As you reflect on your journey, consider what goals you want to set for yourself moving forward. These goals can be academic, personal, or social in nature. Setting new goals can give you a sense of direction and purpose as you continue to grow and evolve.

6. Embracing Change: Reflect on how your attitude toward change has evolved throughout this experience. Embracing change is a valuable skill that can help you navigate transitions and challenges with resilience and optimism. Remember that change is a natural part of life and can lead to new opportunities and adventures.

7. Self-Reflection: Engage in self-reflection to gain deeper insights into your thoughts, feelings, and behaviors. Consider journaling or meditating to explore your inner thoughts and emotions. Self-reflection can help you gain clarity and self-awareness as you continue on your journey.

8. Celebrating Your Resilience: Finally, take a moment to celebrate your resilience and strength in navigating the changes and challenges of changing schools. You have shown courage, adaptability, and determination throughout this journey, and that is something to be proud of.

In conclusion, reflecting on your journey of changing schools is an important step in recognizing your growth, achievements, and personal development. By taking the time to reflect, acknowledge your accomplishments, identify lessons learned, and set new goals, you can prepare yourself for the next chapter in your life with confidence and optimism. Remember that you are strong, capable, and resilient, and that each experience you encounter shapes you into the person you are meant to become.

Understanding How You've Grown

As you reflect on your journey of changing schools, it's important to take a moment to acknowledge and understand how you've grown throughout this experience. Changing schools can be a significant life event that shapes you in various ways, helping you develop new skills, strengths, and perspectives. By recognizing and appreciating your personal growth, you can gain a deeper understanding of yourself and the impact that change can have on your life.

One of the most significant ways in which you may have grown through changing schools is in your adaptability and resilience. Transitioning to a new school environment requires you to navigate unfamiliar territory, adjust to new routines, and interact with different people. In the process, you have likely developed a greater capacity to adapt to new situations, face challenges with courage, and bounce back from setbacks. This resilience is a valuable trait that will serve you well in future transitions and life experiences.

Changing schools also offers opportunities for personal growth and self-discovery. As you navigate the ups and downs of adjusting to a new school, you may have discovered new interests, strengths, and talents that you weren't aware of before. Perhaps you found a love for a certain subject, excelled in a particular extracurricular activity, or forged meaningful friendships that have enriched your life. By exploring these new facets of yourself, you have expanded your self-awareness and gained a deeper understanding of your capabilities and potential.

Moreover, changing schools can foster emotional growth and maturity. Saying goodbye to familiar faces, adjusting to a new social dynamic, and dealing with the uncertainties of a new environment can evoke a range of emotions, from excitement and anticipation to anxiety and sadness. Through these emotional challenges, you have likely developed greater emotional intelligence, empathy, and coping skills. You may have learned how to express your feelings openly, seek support when needed, and empathize with others going through similar experiences. These emotional skills are essential for building strong relationships, managing stress, and navigating the complexities of the world around you.

In addition to personal and emotional growth, changing schools can also catalyze intellectual growth and academic development. Transitioning to a new educational setting exposes you to different teaching styles, curricula, and learning environments, challenging you to adapt your study habits, problem-solving skills, and critical thinking abilities. By embracing these academic challenges, you have the opportunity to expand your knowledge, broaden your perspective, and cultivate a lifelong love of learning. This intellectual growth not only enhances your academic performance but also equips you with the skills and mindset needed to thrive in an ever-changing world.

As you reflect on how you've grown through the experience of changing schools, remember to celebrate your achievements, acknowledge your strengths, and embrace the lessons you've learned along the way. By understanding and appreciating the ways in which this transition has shaped you, you can cultivate a sense of resilience, self-awareness, and personal growth that will empower you to face future challenges with confidence and courage.

Keeping a Positive Attitude Toward Change

Keeping a positive attitude toward change is essential when transitioning to a new school. Change can be daunting and overwhelming, but with the right mindset, it can also be an opportunity for growth and new experiences. In this section, we will explore the importance of maintaining a positive outlook during times of change and provide practical tips on how to cultivate a positive attitude.

First and foremost, it's crucial to acknowledge that change is a natural part of life. Whether it's changing schools, moving to a new city, or starting a new job, change is inevitable and often leads to personal growth. By recognizing that change can bring about positive outcomes and new opportunities, you can shift your perspective from one of fear and uncertainty to one of excitement and curiosity.

One way to maintain a positive attitude toward change is to focus on the benefits it can bring. Moving to a new school presents a chance to meet new people, explore different subjects or activities, and broaden your horizons. Embracing change as an opportunity for personal development and learning can help you approach the transition with a sense of optimism and enthusiasm.

Another important aspect of keeping a positive attitude toward change is practicing self-care and self-compassion. Change can be stressful and challenging, so it's essential to take care of yourself both physically and emotionally during the transition. Make sure to prioritize activities that bring you joy and relaxation, such as engaging in hobbies, spending time with loved ones, or practicing mindfulness and self-reflection.

In addition, maintaining a positive attitude toward change involves staying open-minded and adaptable. Embrace the unknown and be willing to step out of your comfort zone to fully experience all the new opportunities your new school has to offer. Approach challenges with a growth mindset, viewing them as opportunities to learn and improve rather than obstacles to overcome.

Furthermore, seeking support from friends, family, teachers, or school counselors can also help you navigate the changes with a positive attitude. Don't be afraid to share your feelings and concerns with trusted individuals who can provide guidance, encouragement, and reassurance during the transition.

Lastly, remember that change is a process, and it's okay to feel a mix of emotions throughout the transition. Allow yourself to experience and acknowledge your feelings, whether they are excitement, nervousness, sadness, or joy. By accepting and processing your emotions, you can move forward with a clearer mind and a more positive outlook on the changes ahead.

In conclusion, keeping a positive attitude toward change is essential when transitioning to a new school. By recognizing the opportunities for growth, practicing self-care and self-compassion, staying open-minded and adaptable, seeking support, and acknowledging your emotions, you can navigate the changes with resilience, optimism, and a sense of empowerment. Embrace the new school experience with a positive mindset, and you'll be well-equipped to thrive in your new environment.

Looking Forward to New Adventures

Looking forward to new adventures is a crucial mindset to foster as you navigate the transition to a new school. Embracing change and approaching it with a positive attitude can open doors to a world of opportunities and growth.

One of the first steps in looking forward to new adventures is to reflect on the journey you've taken so far. Think about the challenges you've overcome, the friendships you've made, and the skills you've developed along the way. Recognize how far you've come since the beginning of your school change process and acknowledge your resilience in adapting to new environments.

With this reflection in mind, it's important to understand how you've grown through this experience. Changing schools can be a transformative journey that tests your adaptability, courage, and social skills. Consider the ways in which you've become more confident, independent, and open-minded as a result of facing the unknown and stepping out of your comfort zone.

Keeping a positive attitude towards change is essential in fostering a mindset of growth and exploration. Rather than viewing change as a daunting obstacle, see it as an opportunity for self-discovery and personal development. Embrace the unknown with curiosity and enthusiasm, knowing that each new experience brings with it valuable lessons and insights.

Looking forward to new adventures also involves setting new goals and challenges for yourself. Whether it's joining a new club, excelling in a particular subject, or making a positive impact in your school community, strive to push yourself beyond your comfort zone and expand your horizons. By setting ambitious yet achievable goals, you can continue to challenge yourself and unlock your full potential.

Celebrating your progress and success is another important aspect of looking forward to new adventures. Take pride in your accomplishments, no matter how small they may seem. Recognize your efforts and achievements, and give yourself credit for the hard work you've put in to adjust to your new school environment. Celebrating your progress can boost your confidence and motivate you to keep moving forward with a positive mindset.

As you prepare to embark on new adventures in your school journey, remember that you are strong and capable of overcoming any challenges that come your way. Believe in your abilities and trust in your resilience to navigate unfamiliar territory with confidence and grace. Embrace the unknown with a sense of excitement and curiosity, knowing that each new adventure holds the potential for growth, learning, and fulfillment.

In conclusion, looking forward to new adventures is about embracing change with a positive attitude, setting goals for yourself, celebrating your progress, and believing in your own strength and capabilities. By approaching new experiences with an open mind and a sense of optimism, you can turn challenges into opportunities and transform your school change journey into a rewarding and enriching adventure. Embrace the future with courage and enthusiasm, and remember that the best adventures are yet to come.

Remembering That You're Strong and Capable

As you navigate the challenges and changes that come with changing schools, it's important to remember that you are strong and capable. Transitioning to a new school can be a daunting experience, but with the right mindset and self-belief, you can overcome any obstacles that come your way. In this final chapter of the book, we will explore the importance of recognizing your own strength and resilience as you embrace the new school experience.

One of the first steps in remembering that you're strong and capable is to reflect on the journey you have taken so far. Think about the challenges you have faced, the new friends you have made, and the accomplishments you have achieved since changing schools. Recognize the courage it took to adapt to a new environment and the growth you have experienced along the way. By acknowledging your own progress and resilience, you can boost your self-confidence and face future challenges with a positive attitude.

It's also essential to understand that change is a natural part of life and that you have the ability to adapt and thrive in new situations. Remind yourself of past experiences where you have successfully overcome difficulties or stepped out of your comfort zone. Draw strength from those moments and trust in your ability to navigate the unknown with confidence and resilience. By recognizing your past achievements and capabilities, you can approach the future with a sense of empowerment and self-assurance.

As you continue your journey in your new school, set new goals and challenges for yourself. Whether it's joining a new club, improving your grades, or trying out for a sports team, challenge yourself to step outside your comfort zone and push your limits. By setting achievable goals and working towards them, you can build on your strengths, develop new skills, and prove to yourself that you are capable of achieving anything you set your mind to.

Celebrate your progress and success along the way. Acknowledge your achievements, no matter how small they may seem, and take pride in the hard work and effort you have put in. By celebrating your victories, you can boost your self-esteem, stay motivated, and maintain a positive outlook on your abilities and potential.

Lastly, remember that you are not alone on this journey. Lean on your support system of friends, family, teachers, and mentors for guidance and encouragement. Share your challenges and successes with them, seek advice when needed, and draw strength from their belief in your abilities. Surrounding yourself with positive and supportive individuals can help you stay resilient, motivated, and confident in your own capabilities.

In conclusion, as you navigate the ups and downs of changing schools, always remember that you are strong and capable. Reflect on your past achievements, embrace new challenges, celebrate your progress, and lean on your support system for guidance and encouragement. By recognizing your own strength and resilience, you can approach the new school experience with confidence, positivity, and a belief in your own abilities to succeed. You are capable of overcoming any obstacles that come your way and thriving in your new school environment. Remember, you are strong, you are capable, and you have what it takes to succeed.

Printed in Great Britain
by Amazon

52409160R00059